ARCHITECTURAL DRAFTING IN

Mini CAD® 7

for Mac™ & Windows™

The Standard Textbook for Architects, Designers & Builders

JONATHAN STOPPI

ARCHITECTURAL DRAFTING IN MINICAD 7

Qualum (Publishing), P O Box 8722, London NW2 2ZA, UK

British Library Cataloguing-in-Publication Data:

A catalogue record for this book is available from the British Library

Cover design: Lionel Roth

All other illustrations by the author.

Apple and Macintosh are trademarks of Apple Computer, Inc.. MiniCad is a trademark of Diehl Graphsoft, Inc. AutoCad and AutoDesk are registered trademarks of AutoDesk, Inc. All other product names are trademarks or registered trademarks of their respective owners

Printed and bound by The Book Factory, London, England

10 9 8 7 6 5 4 3 2

ISBN 1 899 168 117

Price: £29.95 (US$45.00) nett

To the truly global Apple Computer...

— and other eagerly awaited arrivals

Contents

Working Drawings: Walls & Stuff   49

Symbols   72

Roofs   89

◊

Introduction

My sincerest apologies to all for the delay in getting out this latest edition to the *ADiM* series, due to a combination of overly-ambitious revision plans, unforeseen commitments at business and at home, and an Job-like series of technical hiccups. The good thing to come of it is that I have been able to include information on and demonstrate the first plug-in offering shadow-casting within MiniCad.

And, of course, much else besides. If you haven't upgraded yet from v6, you may wonder, as I did, what on earth could v7 offer, given that MiniCad 6 seemed to cover pretty much all the bases. Automatic formatting of your drawings in HTML for Web publishing?

The answer, it turned out, was 'Plenty'. Some of these features—like the notion of Sheets instead of Views, Recent Files Menu Selection, a simplified procedure for creating custom commands and schedules, Dashed Hidden Line Rendering, and Automatic Wall Join—are sensible, incremental improvements that make work just that little bit easier. Others, however, like an easy, iconic Viewbar at the bottom of the screen, Associative Hatching, Mathematical Expression Input, Dual-Unit Dimensioning, direct AutoCad .DWG Import and Save, the Wall Framer utility, are answers to age-old wishlists that you quickly wonder how you managed without.

These changes are covered in greater detail in the body of our tutorial, signposted as in previous editions with a suitable eye-catching icon to help veteran users spot the areas that they need to focus on to get up to speed with the new version and/or this book.

Otherwise, this edition, like the application, has kept the same basic approach as its predecessors: the reader is not presumed to know anything of MiniCad beyond the essentials of Macintosh™ or Windows™ operation, and is led to learn its tools and methods painlessly and naturally by using them to solve a sequence of familiar problems. The main departures from previous editions are that, in a bid to emulate the design process a little more faithfully, the reader is shown how to create and evaluate a quick sketch design in 2D and 3D before setting down to working drawings, and in so doing covers two hypothetical projects instead of just one to learn about various issues.

Like its predecessor, this edition is 'universal' in that it is equally applicable to both the North American and metric conventions. However, in this edition the roles have switched: English units are the default, with metric equivalents in square brackets ([…]). Where specific references have to be made to one or the other, (North) <u>A</u>merican issues are preceded with the sign @; while readers in the <u>R</u>est of the World are referred to items marked ®.

Square brackets apply also to that other Great Divide, namely between the Mac and Windows versions of the program. In deference to the prevailing cross-section of users, keyboard shortcuts refer by default to the Mac, with Windows equivalents set in square brackets. Most of the screenshots are from the Mac, but where possible the Windows version is used.

A Guide to Graphic Cues & Typefaces

As in previous editions, this book is design in its page size and basic cover binding design to emulate the manuals that come with the application so as to complement them naturally on the shelf. Inside, however, my own conventions apply, namely the main text is in Palatino 10

> *Incidental comments that are not part of the tutorial procedure but worth knowing are in Palatino 9 Italics like this…*

 …—while particularly important points to note are flagged like this.

Issues that require more extensive discussion than is possible in a line or two of text will usually be boxed off in a section of their own, surrounded by a dashed line, and typeset one point smaller than the main text.

 If a warning or and alert is required, this will also be suitably marked

As always, for the sake of clarity (and to avoid excessive use of quotation marks which often confuse more than they help), I use certain fonts when referring to words and figures on screen, corresponding to their appearance under Mac System 7. Thus:
- Menu items and dialog text are set in **Chicago.**
- Screen hints and palette items are set in **Geneva 7 Bold** or Plain as appropriate

- Keyboard operations (e.g. `Shift`, `Option` [`Alt`]) are in the typewriter-like `Courier`.
- The Command key on the Mac is now represented by the icon .

Finally, in response to popular acclaim from previous editions, I have extended and deepened my Ghosted Cursor™ technique of solid gray dots, lines and arrowheads to represent clicks, direction of movement and drag motion, respectively. These should help the reader reconcile screenshots with text instruc-  tions and go some way to making up for the current absence of an instruction CD-ROM or video on MiniCad 7.

Acknowledgments
I am indebted as always to my friend Rafi Shafir for insights on North American practice and for comments on the use of new features such as the Wall Frame. Also:
- to Wendalyn Nichols for advice on American English
- to Thorsten Lemke for his amazing *GraphicConverter*, and to Westcode Software for *OneClick*, —without which this job would have taken even longer
- to Dan Monaghan and everyone at Diehl Graphsoft who answered my questions
- to my MiniCad clients for insights into the program's uses in their work

… and, of course, to you, reader, for your support, which makes the effort worthwhile. I hope the book lives up to expectations. If it does, tell your friends and colleagues. If it doesn't, tell me: a registration form is enclosed at the back for your comments (or use its equivalent posted on the Qualum website at `http://qualum.com/`): please fill this out and return to me with your comments and suggestions, as these will help a great deal in improving the book in future editions. A free copy of my custom AEC Overlay will be sent to all respondents who so wish (see Appendix for details).

Live long and… er, Render.

— JS
London
September 1997

◊

Installation

Windows

Quit all running applications. From the Start pop-up, call up the `Control Panel` dialog.

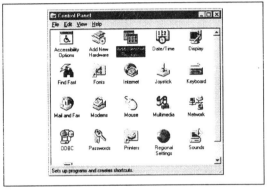

Double-click `Add/Remove Programs`

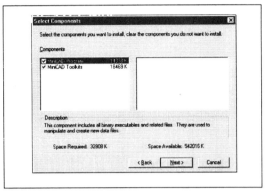

Keep `MiniCad Program` and `MiniCad Toolkits` both checked and click `Next >`

In the `Add/Remove Programs Properties` dialog click `Install...`

In the `Run Installation Program` dialog click `Browse...` (or type the appropriate Command Line if you know it)

/ ...

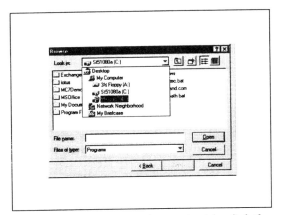

From the Look in: pop-down, double-click the Minicad7 CDROM

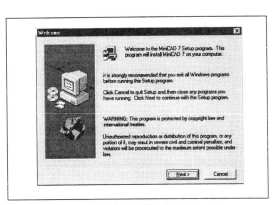

Dbl-click Setup.exe file

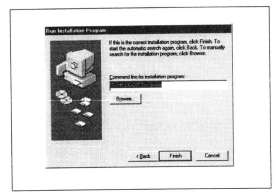

In the **Run Installation Progam** dialog, click Finish

In the **Welcome** dialog, Click Next >

In the **MiniCAD Setup** dialog, click Next> and follow instruction (including entering your details and serial no. from the CDROM cover).

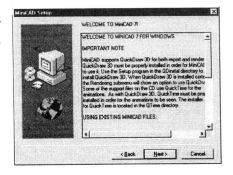

Macintosh

Double-click the **MiniCad Installer** program.

In the dialog, click **Install...** or — to reduce the size of hard disk space necessary for installation — click **Custom**

Pressing the Command (⌘) key to allow non-contiguous selection, click on the options suitable for your machine…

> **Fat Binary** *includes the versions for both PowerPC and 680x0 Macs: this is good when you're installing on an external hard disk that may be used with machines of either specification—otherwise it's not necessary*

… as well as all toolkits you think you will require. Skip the toolkits for Mechanical Engineering and others that you are sure aren't applicable.

Press Enter to or click **Install**

Enter your details and serial number (printed on the CD-ROM cover).

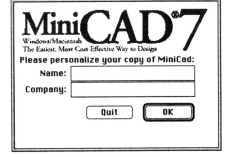

◊

First Acquaintance

The very first time you launch the program, your opening screen should look something like this:

The main difference for MiniCad 6 users is the Viewbar: an array of button at the bottom left of the window: these are shortcuts for common viewing operations: Previous (View), Next (in the series), Zoom in, Zoom out, Normal Scale, Fit to Window, Fit to Object(s), and most important, Saved Views (a pop-up list). More on that later.

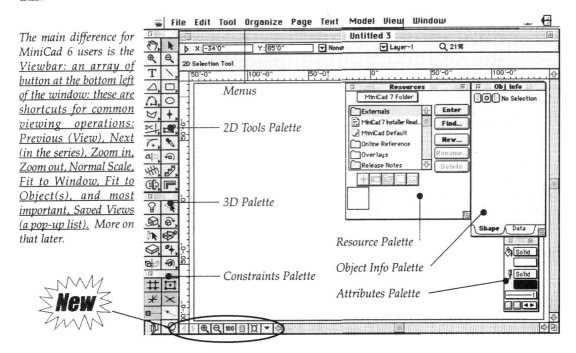

Menus

2D Tools Palette

3D Palette

Constraints Palette

Resource Palette

Object Info Palette

Attributes Palette

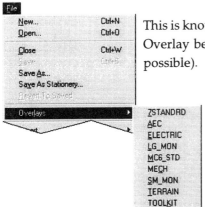

This is known as the **7.x Standard Overlay** [7STANDRD] of the program (an Overlay being a specific arrangement of tools and menus of several possible).

We know this because it says so in the **Overlays** submenu under **File**. We can at any time switch to an alternative Overlay: for AEC work, for large monitors (less crowded), for those still attached to MiniCad 6, etc., by choosing it from the submenu. The list depends on the Toolkits you have installed, and you can even customize your own, using the **Overlay Edit** program that comes with the package, as we shall see later (*see Appendix A*). For now, **Standard** suits us fine, so leave it there.

Setting up for the First Time

The First Five Operations

There are certain other operations that we need to carry out before starting work. MiniCad rightly makes no assumptions as to the type of design intended, so the page size is a single US Letter and the default scale is 1:1. To change this, first choose **Scale...** under the **Page** menu.

The ellipsis (...), by the way, usually means that a dialog box will follow

In the dialog that follows:

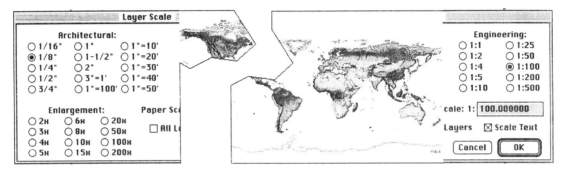

look to the left if you work in the North American [@] system of feet & inches and (for now) choose **1/8"**

look to the right if you're in the Rest of the World [®] for metric/decimal settings and choose the **1:100** 'radio button'

> • *We will use [@] and [®] from here on to distinguish operations or comments for users in North America and the Rest of World, respectively*
>
> • *Being an American program, the heading* **Architectural:** *assumes only Engineers use decimal scales. Note that even when you choose a feet & inches type scale, the* **Paper Scale 1:** *field on the right always displays the decimal equivalent*
>
> • *In your own work, if you don't see the scale that you need from the list of radio buttons (e.g. 1:20), just type it (i.e.,* **20**) *in the* **Paper Scale 1:** *field*

Disregard the **Enlargement** option for now: this refers to the degree zoom achieved by a single click on that tool, and there is no call for it right now.

The next step is to choose your **units of measurement**. By default, these are Feet & Inches: if you need otherwise, choose **Units...** from the same **Page** menu we used earlier. But even if that's what you want, it's worth having a look...

You get the following dialog:

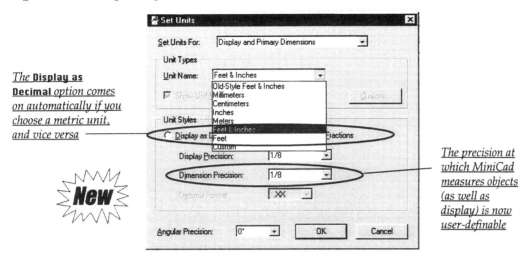

The **Display as Decimal** *option comes on automatically if you choose a metric unit, and vice versa*

The precision at which MiniCad measures objects (as well as display) is now user-definable

Click and hold on the Unit Name pop-up field to see the list of preset options. As in the Overlay submenu, the current setting is always marked with a checkmark. For now,

@:   keep all options at their default settings (**Feet & Inches**, **Display as Fractions** checked, **Round Dimensions to** set at **1/8**)

®:   Choose **Millimeters** (or **Centimeters** or **Meters**, as appropriate) from the list and release to make it the new setting

Note   **Old Style Feet & Inches** *is solely for the benefit of users of very early versions of MiniCad, who wish to import and update old files: don't use otherwise.*

Next, choose your desired precision setting for display & dimension purposes. <u>The two are independent of each other</u>: you can have dimensions measured to an accuracy of a fraction of your chosen unit, but rounded on the drawing to the nearest whole unit, for example.

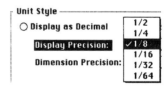

The next operation under the **Page** menu is **Drawing Size....**

This defines the area to be printed or plotted (as opposed to drawing area which in principle can be the extents of your screen).

The standard ISO A, US Arch and other sizes are offered in the dialog's pop-up menu.

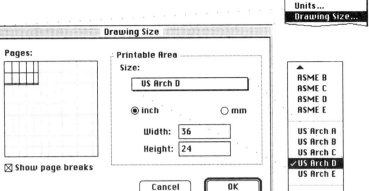

You can also type in the size in mm or inches. You can also opt to show or hide the page breaks in the drawing where your printer or plotter has to divide up the drawing into 'tiles' of smaller sizes. Choose:

@: US Arch D [®: ISO A1]

The size of the 'tiles' are determined by the type of output device that is currently active. If it is a plotter, the plotter driver will have its own characteristic Page Setup dialog, enabling you to get the whole of the chosen size drawing on one tile. If it is an office printer the maximum sizes will be more limited. In any event, you make your choice of size from the pop-up menu and of orientation from the appropriate icons.

Our final step at this point is to set our file Preferences. This is under the **File** menu.

As you can see, MiniCad distinguishes between two distinct types of Preferences: those that affect the particular file we are currently working on (**Document Preferences**) and others — the majority — which relate to the program as a whole and so will affect all files in future (**MiniCad Preferences**). The former are very few and aren't relevant to us right now, referring to options of displaying black & white only or in the colors assigned to particular Layers, and (with 3D objects) how dark to show the new dotted line facility in hidden line rendering.

The **MiniCad Preferences…**, however, are important for us right now in determining many basic aspects of the drawing operation:

There are many things to note here, most of which are self-explanatory and can be left at their default setting. But for our purposes, focus on the **Edit** section only and make sure:

• **Click-drag drawing** option is *off*, and
• **Offset duplications, Screen Hints, Use floating datum** and **Eight Selection Handles** are *on*.

Note, too, the **Dimension Standard** pop-up field for choosing your preferred convention of dimensioning, including those set out by the national

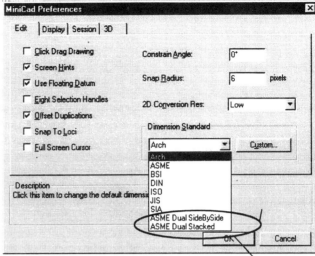

standards of the US (**ASME** – for American Society of Mechanical Engineers – replaces ANSI of old), the UK (**BSI**), Germany (**DIN**), etc. Choose the one your prefer, leave at the default of **Arch**, or make your own customized standard by clicking **Custom…** next to the pop-up…

*The **ASME Dual** options are new and of interest, as they display both English & metric dimensions, as we shall use throughout this book. However, as it is designed mainly to acquaint US practitioners with the metric standard, it always puts metric units in brackets—never the other way around.*

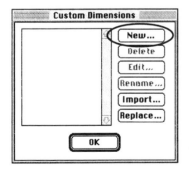

— And in the dialog that follows, clicking on **New**…

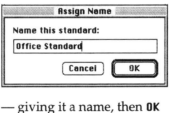

— giving it a name, then **OK** the dialog, and…

Note that you can also import a standard that you have already made in another file: this is a theme that we shall return to

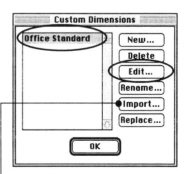

selecting the newly-created standard and clicking **Edit…**

Note the many options available to suit your most exacting requirements as regards type and distance of dimension and witness lines, text, orientation of text, markers, etc.

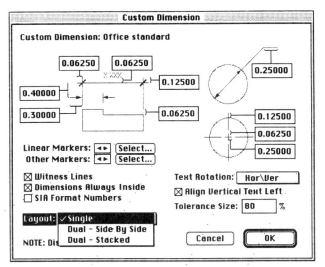

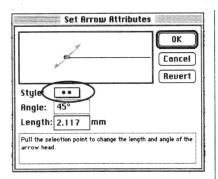

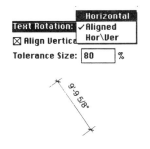

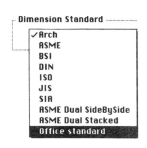

Click on the **Select...** button to change the default markers from the defaults shown to one of the others available in the **Style** pop-up in the **Set Arrow Attributes** dialog. This gives complete control over the size, angle, and appearance of slashes, circles or other markers you may choose.

By default, the text of the dimension is set at the angle of dimension line. When this on a diagonal, however, it can look unclear on the screen, so I personally prefer to set it to be always **Horizontal** or at least **Hor/Vertical** (i.e. whichever is nearest) in all situations.

Finally — a common omission — don't forget to choose your customized Standard from the list back in the **Preferences...** dialog!

The final operation now is to save our file.

Normally, this would be done by simply pressing ⚫ S [Alt+S] or choosing **Save** from the **File** menu, but on this first occasion we want to **Save as Stationery...**

As in other programs, stationery files save your particular combination of settings so that you don't have to go through the same hassle of changing the default settings to your liking each time you create a new drawing file. You will typically create a series of stationery files — one for each kind of size drawing, for example — and then use *them* to launch the application instead of the application icon itself. So far the sort of settings we've made are fairly basic, but as you learn the various features of the program you will be able to (and should) add these, too, to the stationery files, so that all your favorite preferences, commands, symbols etc. are all at hand.

Whenever you ask to **Save as Stationery...** MiniCad suggests the name **MiniCad Default** [default.sta]: accept it, because a file of this name in the application's folder ensures that these settings become the default settings for the program whenever it is launched on its own (there may be an existing file by that name already, in which case, confirm that you wish to Replace it with the new one). But I recommend saving

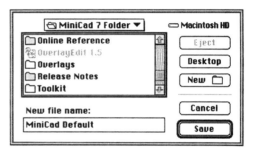

a second copy in a separate folder — perhaps one designated for your future collection of MiniCad stationery — under a more meaningful name that gives information about it, e.g. **@: DL1/8"** [DL8.sta](= Arch D size, Landscape orientation, 1/8" scale) or **®: A1L/100.mm** [A1L100mm.sta] (=A1 size, Landscape orientation, 1/100 scale, mm units).

Stationery file icons look different to their standard counterparts so you can tell them apart straight away, but I sometimes also add a ™ to the name as a kind of private code for 'template'— this helps me identify stationery files at a glance, and to find them easily through the Mac™ or Windows™ file-finding routines.

MiniCad Default 971705A

It is also useful since, unlike in previous versions for some reason, the icons of stationery files now no longer look different from ordinary drawing files in dialogs such as the one above.

Having made the Stationery file, close it or **Quit** [Exit] the program, then double-click on it to create an **Untitled** file, and **Save** that (⚫ S [Ctrl+S]) to practice with. Call it, say, **MiniCad – The Drawing** [MC7Drawing.mcd]

Drawing Tools

The process of drawing in MiniCad — unlike traditional PC CAD conventions, but similar to all native Mac draw-type applications — involves first choosing (clicking on) a tool from the palette, then click-&-dragging or click-move-&-clicking in the drawing area to mark the start and endpoints of the object in question.

On both the 2D and 3D palettes the tools are of three kinds:
• navigation or manipulation of the drawing/model
• object creation or placement
• object manipulation and editing

These are arranged into more or less logical groupings as shown below (more so in the 2D palette than in the 3D). The little arrowhead at the bottom right of some of the tools means that other, related tools or functions are available on a 'pop-out' palette if you click and hold on it (as in the example of the Single Line tool below).

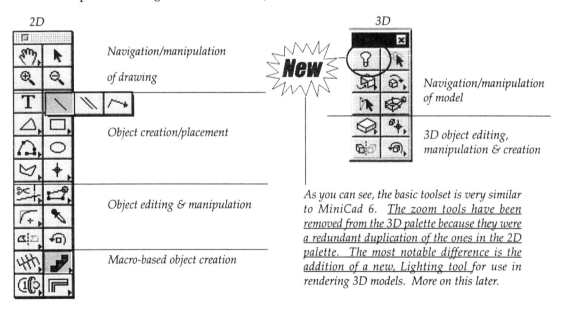

2D

Navigation/manipulation

of drawing

Object creation/placement

Object editing & manipulation

Macro-based object creation

3D

Navigation/manipulation
of model

3D object editing,
manipulation & creation

As you can see, the basic toolset is very similar to MiniCad 6. _The zoom tools have been removed from the 3D palette because they were a redundant duplication of the ones in the 2D palette. The most notable difference is the addition of a new, Lighting tool for use in rendering 3D models._ More on this later.

Experiment using the 2D tools (we'll get to the 3D ones later) to get a feel for the general technique. An in-depth description on each tool is available in the Reference manual that came with your program, but we will also discuss them in detail as well as we go along.

The **Constraints Palette**—as befits its name—allows you to constrain your drawing operations in a number of ways:

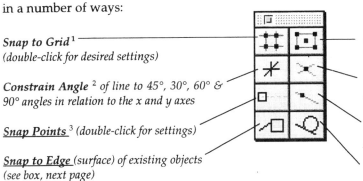

Snap to Grid[1]
(double-click for desired settings)

Constrain Angle [2] *of line to 45°, 30°, 60° & 90° angles in relation to the x and y axes*

Snap Points [3] *(double-click for settings)*

Snap to Edge (surface) of existing objects (see box, next page)

Snap to Object[s] (specifically, their vertices or centers)

Snap to Intersection of any two objects

Snap to Distance [4] *(e.g. a 1/4 length from line end)*

Constrain Tangent (i.e. make a line tangential to an existing circle

---

[1] In the Set Grid dialog you can now create non-symmetrical grids (= different x & y increments) for both snapping & reference purposes. Grids can be displayed and/or printed if you like; and—hurrah!— they can be set at an angle.

Keyboard shortcuts for all options are indicated when the ⌘ [Ctrl] *key is pressed*

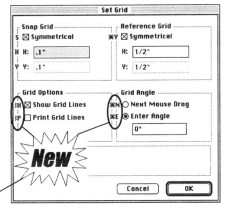

[2] The Angle Snap dialog allows easy & comprehensive control over which angles to constrain a line to in addition to (or instead of) the traditional 30/45/60°. You can also have the angles measured by an Alternate Coordinate System set at an angle to the standard one.

[3] The Smart [Snap] Points dialog offers various options. This constraint must be on in conjunction with Snap to Object for screen hints to be provided.

[4] In Snap to Distance choose between a fraction, percentage, or distance, and whether to make it a multiple division and not just one point from the end.

Where Have All the Constraints Gone?

Those of us who have grown fond of Constrain Parallel and Constrain Perpendicular—stalwarts of previous MiniCad versions—will search in vain for them in the revamped Constraint Palette. The facility is still there, though: its explanation didn't make the main program manuals and it takes some deft mousework, but the payoff is that you can also bisect angles.

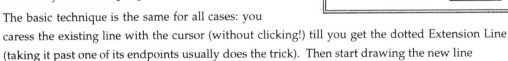

The key lies in the new and slightly mysterious Snap to Edge constraint. More than just a name change for the old Snap to Surface, you use it in conjunction with Snap to Object and Constrain Angle to get parallel, perpendicular, and bisector lines. Double click on the constraint to get its dialog. If it's a bisector you're after, check that checkbox, otherwise check only **Use Floating Edge**.

The basic technique is the same for all cases: you caress the existing line with the cursor (without clicking!) till you get the dotted Extension Line (taking it past one of its endpoints usually does the trick). Then start drawing the new line

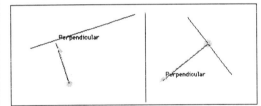

The Perpendicular screen hint appears as you draw (toward or away from the first line) once you're in the vicinity

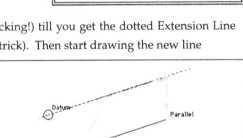

Confirmation of a Parallel line comes, too, with a little more coaxing, once you're nearly parallel

in v7.0.0 it says Edge *instead*

Tick **Snap to Offset** and type in the distance you want for confirmation of a parallel at that Offset

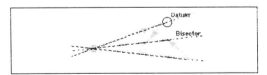

For a bisector, tick **Snap to Bisector** & **Use 2nd Vector**, turn on Snap to Intersection, click at the Intersection and stroke both angle sides before dragging somewhere in the middle.

These constraints are often used in combinations, e.g. Snap to Grid and Snap to Object (the default setting). They are particularly handy when (on the Mac) you know how to call them up 'on the fly', using single-key presses (no ⌘ key necessary) on the lefthand side of the keyboard—leaving the right hand free to draw with the mouse. The ones I find I use most frequently are Snap to Object (press A), Snap to Grid (Q), Snap to Intersection (W) and Snap to Edge (F).

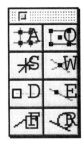

Single-key shortcuts exist for most 2D tools, too. As a guide, use the illustrations to the text superimposition illustrations to the right, but be aware that these can vary: in the AEC Overlay, for example, they're different.

The MiniCad Online Reference

A guide to these shortcuts is provided (Mac only) in the **MiniCad Help** file (Balloon menu), but it has **not** been updated to take into account the changes in the **7.x Standard Overlay** [7STANDRD]. Since in the **AEC Overlay** some of the old shortcuts *do* apply, no single guide is possible, and you should rely on your findings based on trial & error — or do as I do and change the Overlay to your needs (*see Appendix*).

More general help — though mainly in text form— is now provided through a separate file called **MiniCad Online Reference**, running under the Microsoft Help program

> *On Windows, access is through the Help... menu;*
> *on the Mac, it means launching the file which is in its own folder*
> *in the MiniCad folder*

From its startup screen, you can browse through its contents, or **Search** for a specific topic.

The **History** button shows a window where the topics you've looked at are listed in order for easy retrieval. Hyperlinks are provided in the text, too.

There is also a facility to **Annotate** (**Edit** menu) topics with notes of your own to allow you to put the explanation in terms that you and/or your fellow workers can understand.

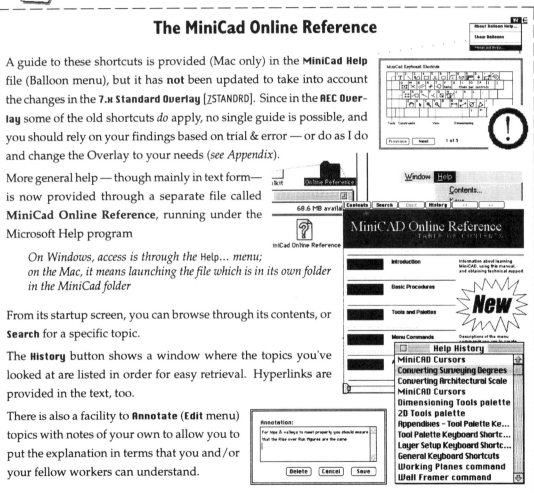

Getting a Handle on Selected Objects

 The Snap to Object constraint is worth going into in some detail as it offers an important insight into how MiniCad (and other draw-type applications) describes objects. MiniCad makes the distinction between two basic types of graphic object:

- Lines
- Surface objects, or objects that describe an area

Line objects are simple: in the mathematical language of programming they are described by just two points— their start and end, respectively.

Line

Surface objects are basically everything else: rectangles, ellipses & circles, arcs of all kinds, Bézier curves and freehand lines, polygons and polylines. The **bounding box** of an object is the imaginary rectangle that just encompasses its entire outline.

Circles made by constraining an ellipse have eight snap handles; made with one of the circle tool options they have only two.

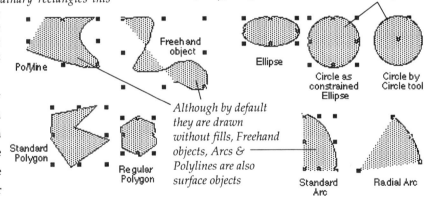

In the case of ordinary rectangles this coincides with the outline of the object itself, but not of course with other objects.

If we were to draw these objects with a visible fill and then select them, we could clearly see how this works for the various types.

Although by default they are drawn without fills, Freehand objects, Arcs & Polylines are also surface objects

In most cases, Snap to Object means that you will snap to the points or vertices of the object. However, with objects with no vertices such as rounded rectangles, circles, ellipses, non-radial arcs, and Bézier curves, what you are really snapping to is to the eight little black square or 'handles' at the corners and the middle of each side of their bounding boxes. A ninth snap-point—

which is invisible—is the center of the object. The exception to this rule are radial arcs (snap points at each end of the arc, plus one at the arc's center; the one in the center of the arc is not a snap point).

The nine points of the bounding box of an object and its center are also used to establish the position of an object in various dialogs. Draw any object with a surface area — e.g., a polygon— and then open up its **Obj(ect)Info** palette (**Window** menu; or press ⌘ I [Ctrl+I]).

Notice the miniature representation of the object's nine handles, one of which is selected (circled).

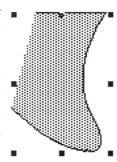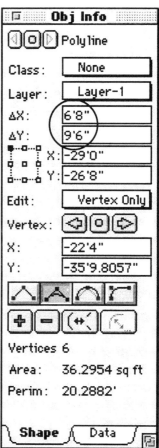

The object's stated position (x and y co-ordinates) are in fact those of the currently selected handle of the object. Click on a different handle in the palette and see how the position coordinates change.

> *This is the why we chose* **Eight Selection Handles** *under* MiniCad Preferences... *earlier: the default option of four handles produces less clutter on the drawing, but wouldn't illustrate the point as well, and would prevent you from resizing by one of the middle handles, which allows us to change one dimension only*

As you can see, the Obj Info palette provides a convenient one-stop-shop for virtually all attributes of a selected object—including Area and Perimeter in the case of surface objects (the word **more...** appears at the bottom righthand corner of the palette if it is too small to reveal all the information). The type of information varies according to the object selected (in the case of polylines, for instance, we can also change the type of each vertex in turn—from point to Bézier curve or cubic spline or radial arc or vice versa). We will discuss the meaning of these attributes as we go along.

Sketch Design

As a good introduction to the 2D palette, let's do some sketch design.

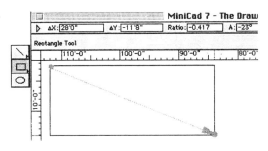

Click on the Rectangle tool, bring the cursor to the drawing area, click to start and drag down and to the right. Note the figures in the Mode Bar changing as you drag. These are monitoring how far horizontally (Δx) and vertically (Δy) you are going in relation to the startpoint, the Ratio between the two, the A(ngle) of the imaginary diagonal you're drawing (in relation to 0°=3 o'clock), and the cursor's current x & y coordinates (note: no "Δ").

> *x and y coordinates are measured in relation to the 0:0 origin of the drawing. This, by default, is its center, but can be changed at any time using the* **Set Origin...** *command (***Page*** menu).*

The nice thing about the Data Display fields is that they are interactive: we can enter the numbers we want *and it will change the object* accordingly. Press the tab key (upper left on your keyboard) to highlight the Δx field and type 23'11 3/8 [7300], and press Enter (Mac-users, note: Enter, *not* Return) to confirm it.

> @: *This is an opportunity to give the lowdown on entering English Units. The foot sign (') is important: without it, MiniCad will assume you mean inches. Immediately after the foot sign, type the inches figure, if any (no need to type a hyphen [-]: MiniCad will format it with a hyphen automatically). For fractions of inches, type a space after the inch figure, and use a standard slash (/). You can also use a decimal notation where this is simpler, e.g. 5'10.75 for 5 '-10 3/4 — the program will do the math.*

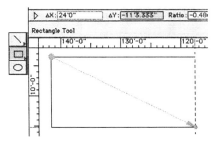

Three things happen at this point:
1. A vertical dotted line has appeared at a horizontal distance of (surprise, surprise) 24'[7300mm] from the startpoint.
2. It is a 'snap-zone': your cursor is free to travel up and down this line, but not sideways. This is ensure that, whatever happens now, your rectangle is guaranteed to have the measurement you entered.

> *This, by the way, is not immutable. If you change your mind or typed the wrong number, no problem. Just press the tab key to highlight each of the Mode Bar fields till it cycles back to Δx, type in the new number, and* Enter *again.*

3. The Δy field is already highlighted, waiting for us to type in a figure for it, too. Type -11'6 [-3500] and Enter.

The minus is important: it tells MiniCad to go down, not up in this case.

Note that the rectangle is now set—having got its Δx and Δy, it's got all the information it needs—and it is selected, in case you'd like to edit it in some way at this point.

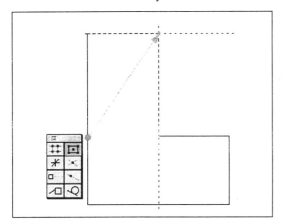

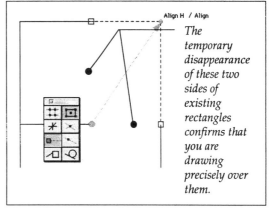

Align H / Align

The temporary disappearance of these two sides of existing rectangles confirms that you are drawing precisely over them.

As it happens, we don't. Instead, by the same method and using Snap to Object on to ensure we start from precisely the first rectangle's upper left corner, we will create another rectangle measuring Δx=12' [3650] by Δy=17'1 [5200].

(No minus necessary this time)

That done, press D to turn on the Smart Points constraint and draw yet another, snapping from the bottom right of Rect.#2, touching (no clicking!) the upper right corner of Rect.#1 with our cursor, then touching Rect.#2's upper right, and dragging to a point aligned with both. When dotted lines appear confirming Alignment with both of these, click to set.

<u>Unlike previous versions, it is no longer enough to have Snap to Object on for the Alignment cues to come on: the new Smart Points constraint must be on, too.</u>

Note

New

Now let's make a circle. Click the Ellipse tool, Circle by Radius option in the Mode Bar, and click at the bottom right corner of Rect#3 (where it meets Rect#1). This time, tab past Δx and Δy directly to L(ength), type 2' [600] and Enter.

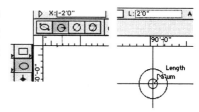

Next, we make a Radial arc.

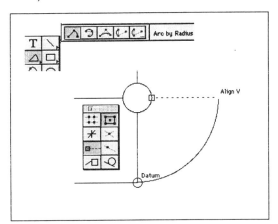

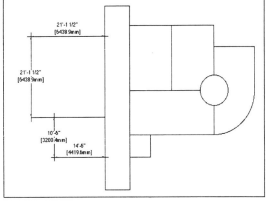

Choose its tool from the palette, keeping the default option setting of Arc by Radius. Make sure Snap to Object and Smart Points constraints are on (keys Q and D). Click at the Center of the circle, drag to the bottom right corner of Rect. #1, and drag up and right to create an counterclockwise arc. When you're aligned with the circle center it should tell you so, in which case click to set.

Chances are the arc's default white fill pattern is now obscuring part of the circle and of Rect#1. To keep things tidy, fix this by keeping it selected and **Send**ing it **to** the **Back**, i.e. underneath the other objects, by choosing the appropriate item from the **Organize**: **Send** submenu .

Now draw a square based on the arc's radius: using the Rectangle tool, click at the end of the arc then touch the circle center momentarily (without clicking) and hold down the Shift key while dragging straight up. When the program confirms you're aligned with the circle's center, click to set. Then make it go 'behind' the circle so as not to obscure it by invoking **Send to Back** (**Tool** menu: **Send**, or keyboard shortcut: B [Ctl+B]).

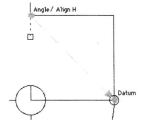

Pressing shift *during click-drag-creation of any geometrical surface object constrains it to symmetrical: rectangles to squares, ellipses to circles, ordinary arcs to radial ones, etc..*

Make another square by the same method starting from the bottom left corner of Rect#1, measuring 5'10 7/8 [1800mm] on either side. Pressing Shift at the same time can feel awkward, but don't worry: you can tab-and-type happily without and only then Shift-and-click to achieve the required effect.

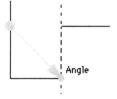

The Floating Datum

We don't always have the convenience of an existing object on the drawing to snap to. Some-times we need to start at a precise distance off. To allow us to do this we call upon a nifty feature in MiniCad called the **Floating Datum**.

This requires that we are about to draw something (or place a sym-bol), and that Snap to Object is on. So, still using the Rectangle tool and with Snap to Object on, touch the upper left corner of Rect#2 and then move away up and to the right. When the word Datum appears next to a small circle surround the point in question, *freeze the mouse* (in fact, let it go). That point is now our temporary datum, or 0:0 point from which x and y coordinates are now measured.

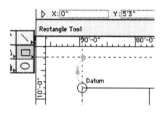

Tab to the x field, type 0 and Enter; then to the y, type 5'3 [1600], and Enter. Dotted snap-lines should appear marking the spot directly 5'3"/1600mm above our chosen point. Click (doesn't matter where, because MiniCad will now start at the meeting of the lines regardless), and drag a rectangle down and to the left. Make its Δx = -7'2 5/8 [-2200], and its Δy=-48'2 3/4 [-14700], and set.

To finish off, make the two last rectangles of the scheme. From the lefthand surface of the long rectangle, at a point aligned with the bottom of the small square we made earlier, drag a rectangle up and left measuring Δx=-14'6 [-4400] & Δy=10'6 [3200], then another on top of it measuring 21'-1 1/2 [6435mm] square (*see next page*).

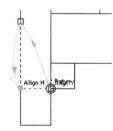

Save your file (⌘ S [Ctrl+S]).

Let the Games Begin

Once you have your basic plan as a arrangement of geometric shapes, it's worth exploring some of the things you can do with them.

For starters, since these are surface-area-type objects and it will help distinguish them against the drawing area, give them a pattern different to the default white fill.

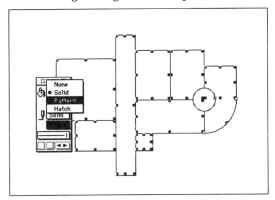 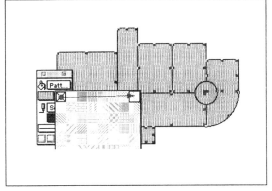

Press ⌘ A [Ctrl+A] on your keyboard to **Select All** objects (**Edit** menu). Then locate your Attributes palette and click-and-hold on the small pop-down menu currently labelled Solid. Choose Pattern instead and release.

A pop-out rectangle appears automatically just below and to the left, showing a default pattern. It's a rather dark one, so click and hold on the pop-out rectangle and choose a lighter pattern from the palette, and release to set.

Clicking on any individual object gives us information about it in the Obj Info palette—information which, like the fields in the Data Display Bar, are interactive with the drawing. Click on the circle, and note the many details known about it (including Area and Perimeter). Select the contents of its Radius field and type 2' [600] instead of the existing setting, and Enter. Note how the circle changes size.

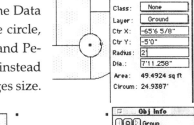

Now select all the objects again and **Group** them (**Organize** menu; or ⌘ G [Ctrl+G]). Note how figures now reflect those of the Group as a whole—including Area & Perimeter, which are true sums of their constituent parts, not of the bounding box.

Very handy during outline planning.

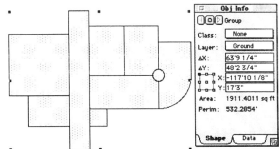

Raising this simple space arrangement into the third dimension is a simple matter.

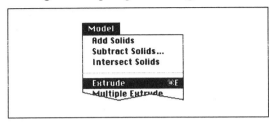

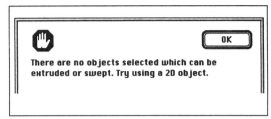

While the Group is still selected, choose **Ex-trude** from the **Organize** menu.

The program says *Na-ah*: the Group is not an Extrudeable object.

> *This raises a general point worth remembering: **a Group is a separate entity from its constituents**—like a corporation is distinct from its shareholders—and as such it is neither 2D nor 3D. We shall see this theme recurring later on in other contexts.*

Not a problem. We could, of course, **Ungroup** it (⌘ U [Ctrl+U]) and start again. But there are advantages to preserving the Group's integrity. So instead, let's 'enter' the Group and Extrude its components from within. Choose **Edit Group** from the **Organize** menu.

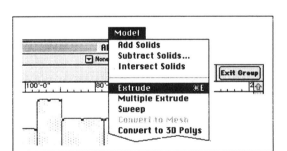

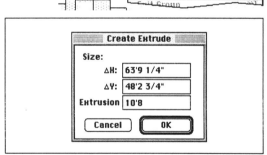

We're now 'inside' the Group: the component items are now individually selected, Layer-1 has been replaced with Group#1, and an **Exit Group** button has appeared on the upper right of the Mode Bar. Now choose **Extrude**

Because we haven't Extruded anything so far in this file, the default value is zero. Assuming that this is not what we want, MiniCad presents us with a dialog inviting us to enter a value of our choice. Type **10'8[3500]**

Note

> *From here on, though, in this file we will have to hold down the* Option *[Alt] key while choosing this item if we want to enter a different value in future. The last extrusion figure used becomes the new default. The exception to this is walls, as we shall see later.*

Notice the objects have lost their fill pattern. This confirms that they have in fact become 3D objects: we are now seeing them in wireframe mode.

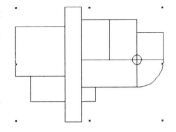

The fill reappears when they are Rendered in a 3D view, as we shall see.

The action of Extruding them all at once has also Grouped them (a Group within a Group, or **nested Group,** as it's known).

To check if it really is 3-dimensional, from the **View** menu, choose
Standard Views>Right Isometric. Unless
you drew the footprints in the dead center
of the drawing, chances are the objects are
off to the side (a MiniCad quirk).
No matter: as they are still selected, if you
double-click either of the Zoom tools or
click on the '100' button (=real-size-as-
printed) at the bottom they will be centered
in the new screen.

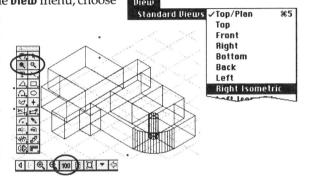

> *Another tip worth remembering if ever you get lost or want to focus on something. If no object happens to be selected,* **Select All** (⌘A [Ctrl+A]), *then use one of these tools.*

Now **Render** it (same menu) to remove hidden lines
and to reveal the objects' inherent fill pattern.

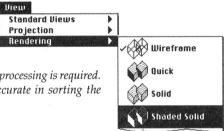

Use one of the options from **Solid** *downwards:
broadly speaking, the further down you go, the more processing is required.
I don't recommend the* **Quick** *option: it's too inaccurate in sorting the surfaces in the right order.*

This is a view we shall probably want to return to for inspection
of our work as we go along, so let's save it.

Click & hold the **Save Sheet...** button at the
bottom left of the drawing window.

This replaces **Save View...** *of previous versions.*

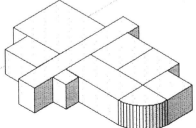

This is also where we'll find it listed later on for future use.

The following rather imposing dialog appears, offering every conceivable permutation of visibility of layers, classes, and other options which don't mean anything to us as yet.

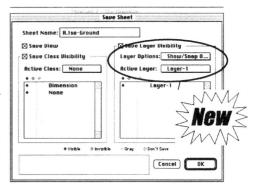

For those familiar with previous versions, this expansion of the old Save View options make it clear why it is now called Save Sheet: through correct manipulation of this dialog virtually any particular project drawing can be recreated in one go. A major contribution to this is <u>the ability now to recall the Layer Options setting of a given view.</u>

Not to worry: for now, using the default settings, just change the name of the sheet from **New Sheet** to **R.Iso.Grd** or some such, and **OK** the dialog.

I find that using a consistent format of [type of view].[level]-[direction] in naming Sheets makes the location of the one you want from the list much easier later on. Caution, however: avoid the use of a slash (/) in the name: MiniCad's internal programming language confuses this with an instruction for a keyboard shortcut, and so it and the first letter that follows it disappear from the Sheet's name in the list.

Back in the drawing, click-&-hold the Save Sheet button and note the view is now listed for future reference.

Now press ⌘ 5 [Ctrl+5] or choose **Standard Views>Top/Plan** to return to the plan view.

*This is not the same as the ordinary **Top** view, which is merely a top view of the 3D model, where—like all model views listed below it—only 3D objects are visible. **Top/Plan** is the actual working drawing, where all objects, both 2D and 3D, various drafting conventions & text can be seen and executed. This distinction is important and will recur later on when we discuss symbols.*

This keyboard shortcut makes it reasonably easy to return to a plan view, but to make it even easier and to ensure that we return to this particular view of the plan at this particular layer, repeat the above **Save Sheet...** procedure and call it **¶-Ground** or similar.

'¶' (Opt-7 on a Mac keyboard) is my shorthand for 'Plan', but of course you can use whatever you prefer.

Save your file.

◊

Layers for Levels (or: Another Storey Altogether)

Time now to create a second level. In MiniCad, as in virtually all CAD packages, this is done by creating a new Layer, which—like an acetate sheet in manual drafting—allows us to draw independently of other levels while keeping them visible if we wish.

Assuming that our upper level will share much of the plan of the ground level, let's first copy what we have there.

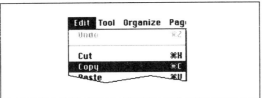

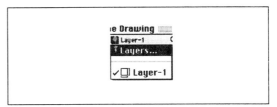

With the Selection tool (the default 'arrowhead' in the 2D tool palette), click on the group of 3D spaces and press ⌘ C [Ctrl+C] (or choose **Edit** menu: **Copy**)

Now click & hold on the little pop-down menu in the Data Display Bar currently labelled Layer-1. Choose **Layers...** to call up the Layers Setup dialog.

The name of the current layer is highlighted: type **Ground** to replace it, then click on the **New** button on the right (or press ⌘ N [Ctrl+N]) to create a new layer. Since the name 'Layer-1' is no longer taken, MiniCad calls this new layer by that name by default. Type **Upper Level** instead and **OK** the dialog.

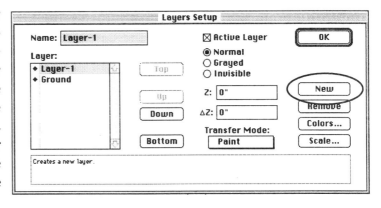

> *In case you're wondering, we're using the terms 'Ground' and 'Upper' to avoid confusion, since '1st Floor' means different things in North America and the rest of the world.*

By default, creating a new Layer and immediately **OK**'ing the Layers Setup dialog makes that layer the current Active one, i.e. the one in which we are drawing. Which means we should now be in Upper Level. This should be confirmed by the label of the Layers pop-down menu, which should now say Upper Level. (If it doesn't, click-&-hold the label's arrow-head and choose **Upper Level** from the list). Note that the Active layer is always the one with the checkmark.

Another sign that we are now in the Upper Level layer is that the objects in the Ground layer are grayed out.

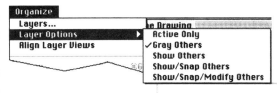

This is due to another default, which is that **Layer Options** (**Organize** menu) is set to **Gray Others**. We'll explore the other options later on. For now, note that the Ground collection appears as a plain rectangle (that of its bounding box). This is because it is a Group, and Groups are treated as one object when viewed in **Gray Others** mode from other layers.

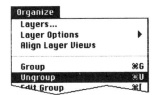

To make the group components visible from other layers in Gray mode, return to the Ground layer by choosing it from the Layers pop-down menu, select the collection and **Ungroup** it (**Organize** menu, or ⌘U [Ctrl+U]).

Now if you return to the Upper level layer (same method) you will see the individual objects defined as gray objects. Press ⌘v [Ctrl+V] to **Paste** (**Edit** menu) the collection we copied earlier. Chances are you will get something like this (see right), i.e., they don't quite match.

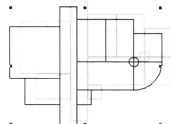

That's because we didn't **Paste in Place**, which is MiniCad's way of ensuring that objects are put down at precisely the same coordinates they had when they were Copied. Delete (select-&-backspace-key) the just-pasted collection, and this time choose **Paste in Place** (**Edit** menu) or press Option-⌘-V [Ctrl+Alt+V]. The collection is now pasted in precise registration with their counterparts at Ground level.

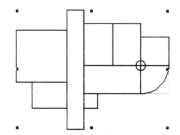

> *The keyboard shortcut uses V and not P key because ⌘ P [Ctrl+P] is reserved for the* **Print** *command (***File** *menu), as in all native Macintosh applications.*

The Obj Info palette as an editing tool

Let us now make some changes to the Upper Level spaces. To see the results more clearly in 3D, let's view them in a Right Isometric view as before. But this time, instead of going via the **Model>Standard Uiews** menu, take a shorter route:

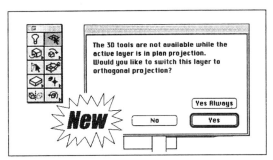

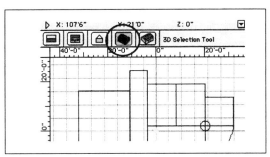

Click on the 3D Selection Tool in the 3D palette. This immediately calls up a dialog pointing out that 3D tools are not available in the Top/Plan (=working drawing) projection. To avoid getting this dialog every time in future, (which can be a nuisance) click **Yes Always**

> *The absence of such an option in previous versions was a major disincentive to using it*

We're now in ordinary **Top** view. To get the Right Isometric view, all we need to do now is click on the Mode button second from right.

> *The others, as can be inferred from the icons, are (from left) Top, Front, Side & Left Isometric*

Another favor we could do ourselves is temporarily to remove the Reference grid that interferes with the legibility of the wireframe.

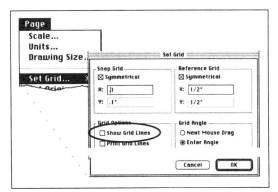

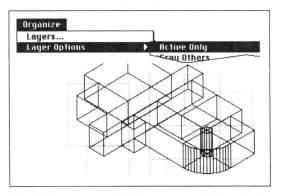

Choose **Select Grid...** (**Page** menu), uncheck the **Show Grid** option, and **OK**.

The objects are much clearer now, although the gray outlines of the Ground layer objects are still visible. To remove these, choose **Active** [Layer] **Only** from the **Layer Options** menu.

We're now ready to start editing the objects. First Ungroup the collection so that we can access the individual spaces.

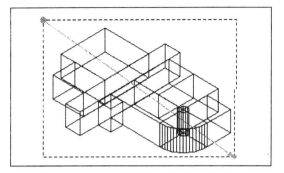

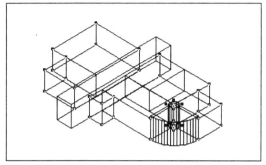

Then with the 2D Selection tool (the default 'arrowhead' tool in the 2D palette), click-drag-release an imaginary rectangle or marquee encompassing all the objects (so-called as the dotted line runs around like the lights of theatre marquees).

With all the objects thus selected, hold down the Shift key and click on the long rectangular box (forming the upper part of our intended corridor) to deselect it individually.

That's how you deselect a single item within a collection of selected objects

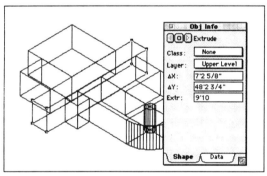

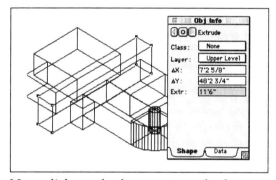

Now call up the Obj Info palette if it isn't open already (**Windows** menu—or I [Ctrl+I]). Because all the selected objects share the same Extrusion value, it is displayed on the palette. Highlight this value and type 9'10 [3000] instead, then press Enter. The objects shrink on cue.

Now click on the long rectangular box we deselected earlier. It becomes the only selected object (because we weren't pressing Shift), and the Obj Info displays its measurements. Highlight its Extrusion value and change it to 11'6 [3505], and Enter.

Render the scene **Shaded Solid** to check the result and **Save Sheet...** as **R.Iso.Upper** or similar.

Now things begin to get interesting. Click to select the quarter-circle object: this is intended to be a balcony. Highlight its Extrusion value and change it to 3'4 [1000].

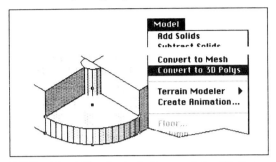

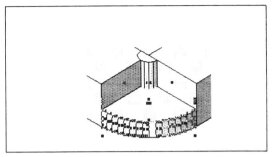

While it's still selected, **Convert to 3D Polys** (**Model** menu). The pattern of selection handles changes subtly: from a standard 3D extrusion it is now a Group of discrete 3D polygons.

To reveal these, **Ungroup**.

The concept of a 3D Polygon is an important one. These are polygons of no thickness, and yet they are of a '3D nature' because their coordinates are defined in three dimensions within MiniCad. Thus they can be seen and manipulated within one of the 3D views, whereas a standard 2D object drawn in Top/Plan cannot. This distinction, too, will recur later when we discuss symbols.

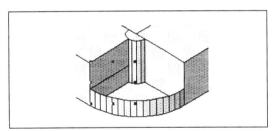

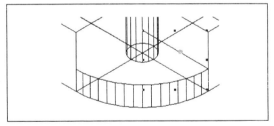

Select the top surface polygon ('lid') and delete it to reveal the hollow. Do the same to the left rear polygon as shown.

If we return to a **Wireframe** Render for a moment, we can see its right-rear companion: delete it, too.

To keep things tidy, draw a marquee around what's left (taking care not to take in any of the surrounding extrusions) and Group them.

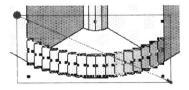

One need not necessarily delete 3D polygons to gain a hollow effect: one can simply remove their fills, instead. Thus, to achieve the effect of a handrail, for example, **Edit** the **Group** that we've just made, and draw a marquee around the polygons of the vertical stand to select them.

Note that Rendering doesn't occur within Groups. All editing must be done in wireframe, with the results viewable when you Exit

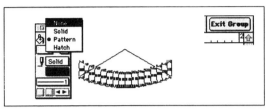

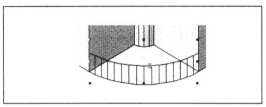

Although we can't see the fill-pattern, MiniCad knows that they have one. In the Attributes palette, choose None from the pop-up menu to remove all fills. Then **Exit Group.**

The result can be seen in the Rendered model.

Practice the same technique to make hollow handrails from the two adjacent extrusions.

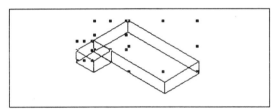

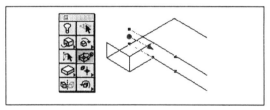

This time, though, carry out the **Convert to 3D Polys** operation on the two together. This ensures they are Grouped together, which allows you (once you **Edit Group**) to pull back the 'handrail' facet of the long box to the point

where it meets its counterpart on the small one. This 'pulling back' is carried out with the **3D Reshape Tool**, by dragging on the middle handle so that you don't distort the shape of the rectangle.

A very useful tool. We'll return to it later.

OK. We're just about ready to put the two storeys together into one integrated model with which to examine our handiwork so far, but before we do:

• Select the long corridor rectangle and change its height to 12' [3660].

• Change the cylindrical object (intended to be a circular chimney) to a height of 14' [4270].

Save your file.

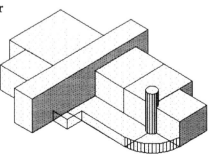

Making an Integrated Model

At this point, we can view either of the levels from any angle we want, but we have no way of viewing them together as an integrated two-storey structure as intended. We could, of course, take either layer, view it in, say, Right Isometric, choose **Organize : Align Layer Views** to ensure

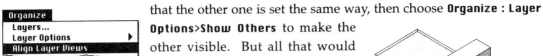

that the other one is set the same way, then choose **Organize : Layer Options>Show Others** to make the other visible. But all that would achieve is the two occupying the same space, creating a meaningless, single-storey mishmash:

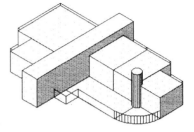

To solve this, MiniCad uses a method known as **Linking Layers**. This works on the principle that you create a new layer, dedicated to the integrated model, which is told, in effect, *'Take the contents of layer B and show them placed on top of the contents of layer A so that layer B starts where A ends'*. The procedure is as follows:

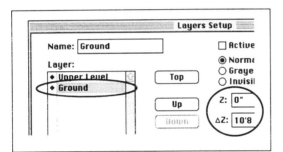

Go into Layers Setup dialog, select the **Ground** layer from the list. Keep its **Z** (the height at which it 'starts') at zero, but set its **ΔZ** (the height of the layer, i.e. the distance between its 'floor' and its 'ceiling') to the value that we Extruded its space objects earlier: **10'8 [3500]**).

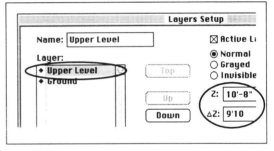

Then select the **Upper Level** from the list and set its **Z** to the sum of the Ground level's **Z** and **ΔZ**, i.e., 0+10'8"=10'8" [3500]. Then set its **ΔZ** to the value that we extruded most of *its* objects, i.e., **9'10"[3000]**

This highlights an important point: the 'ceiling' set by the ΔZ of a layer is not an impenetrable 'force field': individual objects in the layer, like the chimney stack and corridor in the Upper Level, can be set to exceed it. The ΔZ merely establishes the vertical extent of a layer so that the integrated model knows how to stack them one on top of the other. It also sets a convenient default height for walls and newly Extruded objects.

Now create a new layer called **Model**. Notice it starts where the last one left off, i.e. it automatically assumes a starting height (**Z**) equivalent to the sum of the **Z** and **ΔZ**s of the existing layers. It also assumes you want it to have the same **ΔZ** as the previous layer.

This would normally be convenient, but as they are not needed and will only interfere with the settings of future layers, zero them both. Also, mark this layer **Invisible**, so that it is not visible from other layers when **Layer Options** is set to one of the **Show Others** options (in most instances it will get in the way)

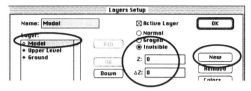

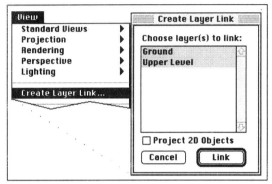

Back in the drawing, choose **Create Layer Link...** (**View** menu). In the dialog, press Shift and click on both **Ground** and **Upper Level**, and **OK**.

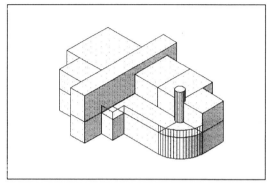

The result (in **Right Isometric**) should be something like this, showing the two levels arranged as intended. Congratulations. **Save Sheet...** this view: we will return to it often.

Now that we have a basic design to look at, let's check it out from various angles.

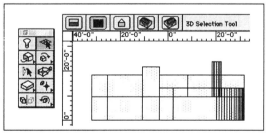

Click the 3D Selection Tool and click on the Front button. **Save Sheet... (as**, say, **ΣModel: Front**, where **Σ**=Elevation).

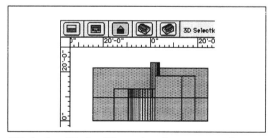

Click the Right Elevation button, and **Save Sheet...** it, too.

Perspectives & Walkthroughs

There are many ways to get a perspective view of a 3D object or model in MiniCad. One of the easiest but often overlooked ways is to start from an orthogonal one. This one-step switch is particularly useful when evaluating or demonstrating designs which may give quite different impressions in true perspective vs. strict orthogonal elevations.

Change our **Standard Views>Projection** from **Or-thogonal** to **Perspective**.

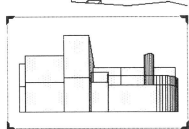

> *You can always tell you're in a Perspective view because it's in a frame with old-fashioned 'picture-holders' at the corners. The frame itself can't be moved as an object, but the picture-holders can, in order to see more or less of the scene.*

The new Projection setting holds until further notice for all new 3D views (not Saved Sheets: that would defeat their purpose). So now if we switch to a **Front** view (either through **Standard Views** menu or by clicking the Front mode button of the 3D Selection Tool), we'll see it, too in perspective:

Notice we're seeing the ground straight on. That's because the default is to view the object/model in question at the level of its starting **Z**. We're also standing at a certain default distance. (**Save Sheet...** these views.)

Both these parameters can be changed dynamically through use of the **Walkthrough Tool**. It has a number of modes al-

lowing us (as the icons show fairly plainly) to move up, down, or look up or down. But in fact you'll hardly ever use them. Instead, you click-&-hold the mousebutton and keep the cursor

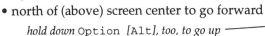
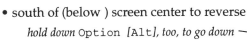

- north of (above) screen center to go forward
  hold down Option *[Alt], too, to go up*
- south of (below) screen center to reverse
  hold down Option *[Alt], too, to go down*
- left of center to pan left
- right of center to pan right

Practice using the Walkthrough Tool without Option [Alt] for a bit to get the hang of it. To walk around to see the building from another angle, for example, pan to the left or right, then move forward, then pan back to the building. To speed things up, press `Shift` while you move. If you get lost (which can easily happen), click on the last button in the Mode Bar: it takes you back from wherever you are to the original **Front** view so you can start again.

Aspects of Walkthroughs

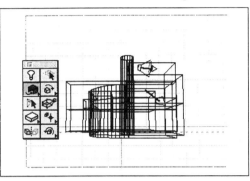

Press `Option` [Alt] to go up or down.

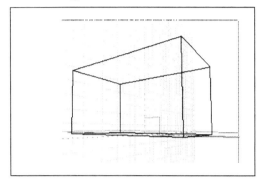

Pressing `Shift` speeds things up by switching from wireframe to bounding-box display

Preparing for the working drawing

In the run-up to starting our proper drafting, we move back to a plan view of the Ground level. For this we take advantage of the Saved Sheet we made earlier by selecting it from the Saved Sheets list pop-up.

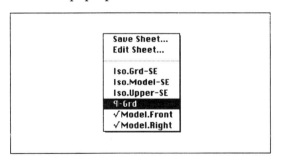

But there's a problem. What we get is a mixed view, where we're in the Ground level alright

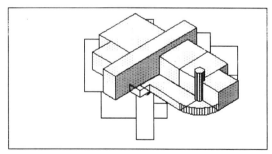

and seeing it in **Top/Plan** projection, but the **Right Isometric** of the Upper level is superimposed on top of it.

The little icon next to the Upper Level layer in the Layers pop-down confirms that it is set to Normal. This is because it didn't exist when the **¶-Grd** Sheet was Saved, and no one told it how to behave in that Sheet once it came into being—so it is now as it was when we last left the Layers Setup dialog.

The little isometric cube also tells you that it is currently in one of the 3D projections, as opposed to Top/Plan as in the case of the Ground level.

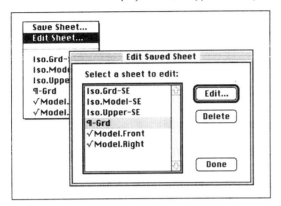

To fix this in all future callups of **¶-Grd**, choose **Edit Sheet...** from the pop-up, then double-click on the errant Sheet in the dialog that follows.

In the Edit Saved Sheet dialog, click in the hollow diamond (=Invisible) column for both the Model and Upper Level layers to replace their current setting of Don't Save, and **OK**

Don't Save *is short for 'I don't care whether it's visible or not: use whatever setting is currently going for that particular layer'.*

Note that we could also change the Layer Options setting to **Active Only** *— but that would prevent us from displaying other layers that we* **might** *want to see later, like the Titleblock, Site Plan, etc.*

Back in the drawing, we see the Ground spaces on their own, as intended.

Save your file.

New

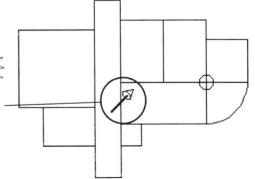

In case you're wondering, the little 3D arrow objects represent the default type of light source that is created automatically the first time you Render in a given Layer. They appear in all 3D wireframe views, but can be turned off in the MiniCad Preferences dialog if you prefer. More on them later.

Working Drawings: Walls & Stuff

With a basic design to work from, it's time to do some proper drafting. As you may have already noticed, <u>MiniCad lists the files last worked on in the File menu for easy access.</u> Use it to reopen our fi'

Click on the **Wall Tool**

Keyboard shortcut: 9 — does not work in the Standard Overlay.

Notice how, when you do so, a number of options appear in the Mode Bar:

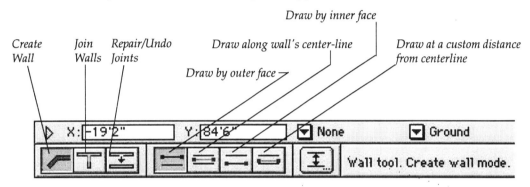

Create Wall | Join Walls | Repair/Undo Joints | Draw by inner face | Draw along wall's center-line | Draw at a custom distance from centerline | Draw by outer face

• The first three are about whether you are creating, joining, or 'cleaning up' a wall

• The next four relate to how you are drawing the wall: by the inner face (assuming a clockwise motion), the outer face, its centerline or perhaps a certain distance offset from the centerline.

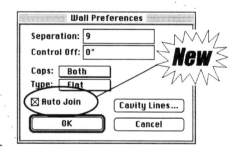

• The last item is a button which calls up the **Wall Preferences** dialog. This is where basic attributes of the wall are set, such as overall thickness (**Separation**), method of 'capping' (whether it ends with a flat line, a round one or none at all), whether it is one leaf or a composite or cavity wall, etc. <u>**Auto Join** ensures that a wall segment will automatically join to the end of an existing one on the drawing</u>: make sure it is on for now.

These options all hint at the fact that the Wall Tool does more than just draw a double line, but several operations all wrapped up in one (in effect, a kind of **macro**). Each wall segment is in fact a sophisticated Group of lines and fills that not merely works as one but responds 'intelligently' to junctions with other walls and inserted items such as windows and doors. It is also a hybrid 2D/3D object, with an automatic height size (ΔZ)—that of the Layer in which it is created in at the time of its creation.

All of which we shall see later. For now, in the Wall Preferences dialog,

- Type **9 1/4[230]** in the **Separation** field
- In the **Caps** pop-up field, select **Both**

> *This closes off wall sections at either end where left open. Ignore* **Control Off** *for now – irrelevant for our purposes*

- Make sure **Type** is set to **Flat**

> *Round caps don't join well at L- or T-type junctions*

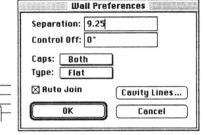

By clicking on the **Cavity Lines...** button, we can also make a custom cavity wall to our requirements, but we won't bother with that at this scale (see box). **OK** these settings.

The next bit is optional, but I find it useful to give the walls a very light color: enough to be distinct against the white background, but light enough to feature dark selection handles

> *Traditionally one might think of using a pattern of some sort—or even a black fill—but these carry through to the walls' rendering in 3D views and can interfere with the legibility of the general model*

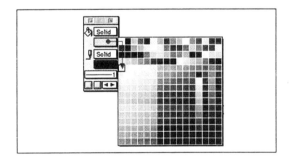

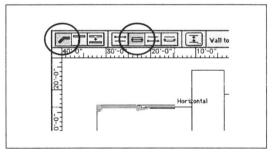

Call up the Attributes palette, choose Solid from the 'bucket' (surface-object-fill) pop-up, then click-&-hold the rectangle under it and choose a very light, neutral color.

> *Pre-selecting a fill or Pen attribute in this way before we start drawing makes it the new default for all new objects.*

With our wall settings now ready, snap to one of the corners of the existing space objects and, as you drag the cursor, press the or I key (on Macs: the ⌘ key, too, will work) once to change mode of drawing from the default top face to drawing-by-centerline, as shown.

Note the Data Display Bar is monitoring your movements as you drag just as it did earlier with the rectangles and other shapes. Had we not any existing objects to snap to, we would tab-&-type the measurements of these wall segments in exactly the same way. But with these objects

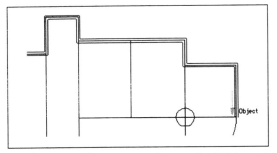

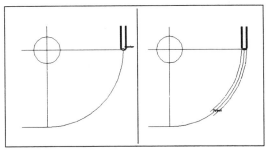

in place, just keep snapping and clicking at each corner of the external envelope until you get to the start of the curved wall. Double-click at that point to terminate the wall chain.

Anything other than a double-click will keep the chain going indefinitely...

Zoom in on the arc so that we can snap more easily to the joints of its component segments. As you bring the cursor to the end of the last wall section, the latter thickens in anticipation that you wish to **Auto Join** to it. Click at that point, then snap to each point labelled Object along the arc: these correspond to the segment joints.

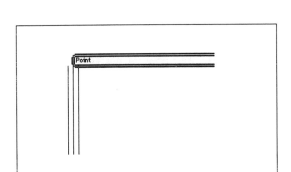

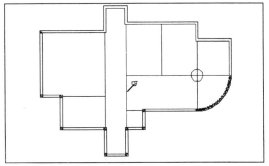

Carry on the straight sections afterwards, and, when you arrive back at the point at which we started its segment, too, thickens. Click to join automatically.

The final result should look something like this.

Note: wall chains remain selected immediately after creation: useful in case they've come out wrong and you want to delete them.

In preparation for creating the internal walls, go back into Wall Preferences and change Separation to **4 [100]**.

On Making Cavity Walls

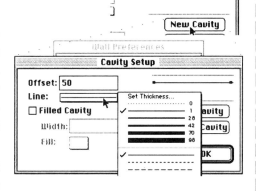

Click once on the **New Cavity** button…

A cavity line appears, with handles at each end indicating that it is selected, ready to be told what to be and where to go. In the **Offset** field type 2"[®:50]. Also, click-&-hold on the **Line** pop-up and note how you can choose a suitable line thickness (to distinguish it from the outer faces of the wall, which might be thicker).

Click anywhere in the white area of the dialog (don't press Enter: this would confirms the setting but also dismiss the whole dialog) and note the line moves into position.

> *The measurements in the Cavity Setup are made in relation to the wall's centerline. This requires a little mental arithmetic: if, for the sake of argument, you want an outer leaf of 2" (50mm) in a wall whose total thickness (**Separation**) is 9" [say, 250mm], you calculate that, in relation to the centerline, the inner face of the outer leaf must be offset $9 \div 2 - 2 = 2.5"(250 \div 2 - 50 = 75mm)$.*

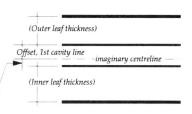

(Outer leaf thickness)

Offset, 1st cavity line

imaginary centreline

Offset, 2nd cavity line (negative figure if below centerline)

(Inner leaf thickness)

Now click **New Cavity** again and type -1 [25] in the **Offset** field. (Being below the centerline, the figure is negative.) **OK** the dialog.

> *Cavity components can optionally be fills instead of lines — to represent insulation, for example. This is triggered by turning on the **Fill Cavity** option, whereupon the **Width** and **Fill** fields are activated. The fill object is an open-ended rectangle (i.e. with only top and bottom faces drawn): type in the width and give it the fill (or hatch) of your choice from the pop-up. For its positioning, note that the offset here refers to its inner (bottom) face: to illustrate, note here how a 2 1/2" [60mm] fill object relates to the previous two cavity lines when placed at zero offset.*

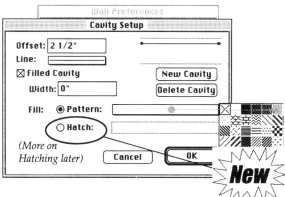

(More on Hatching later)

Incidentally, you are not limited to only four lines: walls can have any number of lines and/or fills. In addition, you can select a cavity line/fill and change its parameters retroactively at any time.

Drawing internal walls works much the same way. Here the issue is the relationship to the external walls:

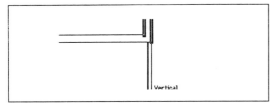

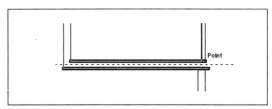

in particular, changing the face by which you draw to be flush with an internal corner, etc. To ensure the right result, it's best to work closer up than the overall plan. If the screen

runs out before where you want to go, just keep going: the screen will follow as your cursor pushes against its boundary.

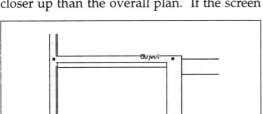

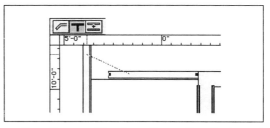

Although Auto Join is handy, it can occasionally cause unintentional joints by 'guessing' wrongly which section you wish to join to. To fix things, you'll need to delete the new wall

section, then pull back on the section that went too far, and rejoin it with its original partner. For this, you use the Join wall mode, and click first one then on the other

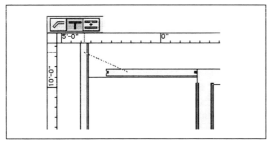

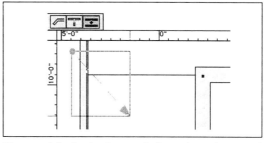

With Auto Join off, stop the new section short, and do the same with it and its target. Alternatively, select the two sections in question (and only them), and press ⌘ J [Ctrl+J] (short for choosing **Tool >Join** menu command).

To mend 'holes' where a defunct junction used to lie, use the Wall Tool in its third Mode—Remove wall breaks/caps—and draw a marquee around the affected area.

When drawn around an existing junction, this disconnects wall junctions

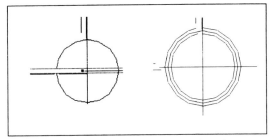

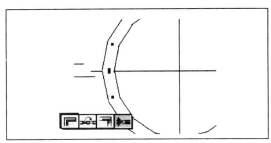

We use the Wall Tool to create the chimney piece, too, tracing over the segments of the 16-sided polygon created when the original circle was Extruded—but only after drawing back the corner walls. Each of these is then Joined with the nearest chimney segment.

Where a 3-way join is required, we select two of the segments, then invoke the Y-joint Tool (from the Wall Tool series) and click with it on the third.

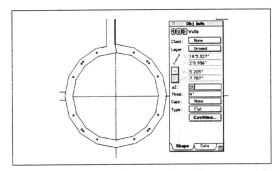

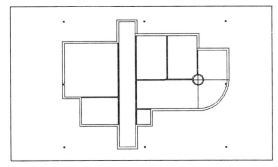

It remains only to Shift-select the two middle segments in each of the four quarters of the chimney piece, call up the Obj Info palette and reduce their Δz to 20"[500]. When done, Group them as well for easy selection later on.

Zoom out in the plan and click on one of the exposed boundary lines between the space object to select their entire Group —and delete. They're no longer needed and will only get in the way of the model.

The result—as our R.Iso-Grd Saved Sheet should show—should be something like this.

Repeat the process in the Upper Level layer and save your file.

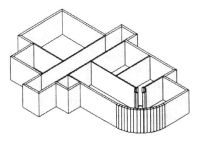

◊

Custom Visibility...

Or: How to Make Certain Objects Come and Go Away As and When Required

When you finish creating the walls in the Upper Level you will find it not quite as easy to get rid of the space objects as in the Ground floor layer. That's because we Ungrouped the latter for easier access to individual objects for editing.

Of course, we could just **Send to Back** each wall as wze go along, but wouldn't it be nice if we could just hide all the walls temporarily in one go, just until we deleted the space objects? Well, **Custom Visibility...** allows us to do just that. With it, we can hide, show, or show only all sorts of objects on the drawing based on criteria such as Name, Symbol, Layer, even Line Style, Weight, etc.

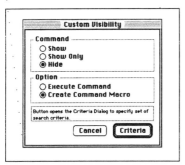

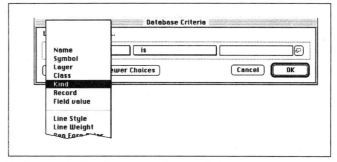

In the first dialog that comes up, select **Hide** and **Create Command Macro**, then click **Criteria**

In the next dialog choose **Kind** from the left pop-down list, leave the second list set to **is**, and select **Wall** from the list that replaces the text field to the right

OK'ing this creates a **Command** which you can invoke at any time later to hide such objects: call this one **Hide Walls**, &**OK**.

A new palette appears which will list all new custom Commands that you make in due course. Double click on Hide Walls to hide the walls in the Upper Level, and delete the space objects. To bring the walls back, repeat the procedure, only this time choose **Show**, name the Command as such, then use it.

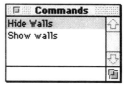

In situations where what you want to do is probably just a one-off, one would choose the default **Execute Command** *instead of* **Create Command Macro** *in the first dialog.*

Stairs & Such

Now that we have two storeys, a means to get from one to the other might be in order.

MiniCad makes this task a little easier by incorporating a special **Straight Stair Tool**. This semi-automates the process by producing ready-made flights of stairs in 2D and/or 3D, to our specifications.

The explicit inclusion of the word 'Straight' suggests that in future versions other types of stairs will be available. And in fact a special MiniCad External for other types is already available from a 3rd party developer: see the Graphsoft Dispatch for details

 After choosing the tool from the 2D palette, change its default Modes to drawing-by-the-right-stringer and by the rear of the landing. Then in the Preferences dialog:

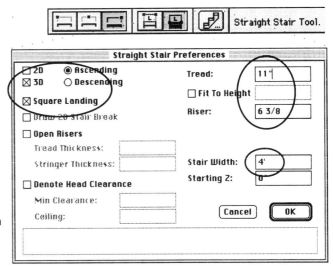

- select the **3D** and **Square Landing** options
- change **Riser** to (10'8"÷20=) **6.4"** **[162.56]**
- deselect the 2D checkbox
- leave **Tread** depth and **Stair Width** at their defaults (11", 4") and **OK**.

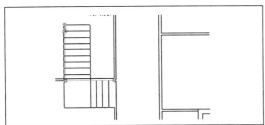

Square Landing means we can do two landings at once. Pressing Shift to constrain to the horizontal, start from the inside corner as shown, drag out four full treads before click-&-dragging up another nine. Click once to set.

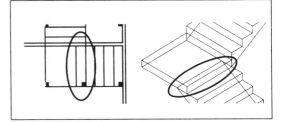

You'll note an extra line under the landing. This is not a mistake or a bug, but the underside of the last tread as seen in a Top view wireframe mode of the 3D object, as an Isometric view will show.

To hide this and generally make it more appropriate to a working drawing, we now trace over what we've done in 2D mode.

The two can be done at the same time by turning on both 2D and 3D options in the Stair Preferences — but doing them separately illustrates the issues and also gives us more flexibility in editing later

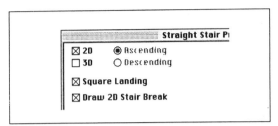

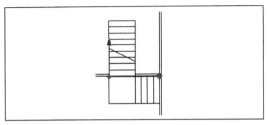

In the Stair Preferences, turn off **3D** and turn on **2D** and **Draw 2D Stair Break.** & **OK**

Back in the drawing, trace over what we did earlier and click once to set. Note the stair break.

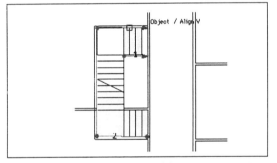

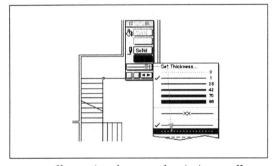

Next draw the final flight of five steps starting from the topright corner of the 3D flight. This is purely as a guide for the new walls which should now be drawn hugging the stairs from all three sides: the actual third flight will be created in the Upper Level layer, so once the

new walls are in place, and existing walls retracted and joined up accordingly, delete the new steps from the drawing. To depict them as an overhead element, however, draw a line and—through the Attributes palette—make it a broken one.

We're ready to make the necessary amendments to the Upper Level. But before we do, let's make the job of distinguishing between elements on the two floors easier by color-coding them.

Color-coding layers is usually associated with traditional CAD systems like AutoCad which use a black background. But it is no less useful here, too, whenever we are viewing other layers, particularly as it avoids having to change the actual attributes of existing and future objects in those layers.

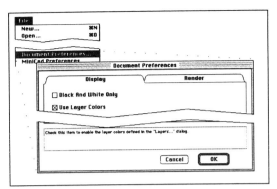

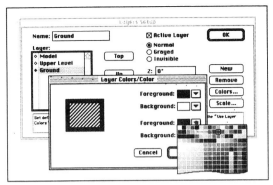

Choose **File : Document Preferences...** and turn on **Show Layer Colors** in the default (**Display**) panel. **OK** the dialog, then go into the Layers Setup dialog (**Layers...**).

Click once on the Ground Floor layer from the list then click **Colors...**. In the dialog that follows, click-&-hold on the lower (Pen) **Foreground** pop-down square and choose, say, a green instead of the default black.

OK that, then select the Upper Floor layer and repeat the procedure, choosing a different color this time. And **OK** the Layers Setup.

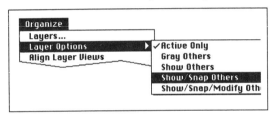

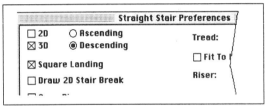

In the Upper Level layer, set **Layer Options** to **Show/Snap Others**.

In the Stairs Preferences dialog, turn on **Descending** and **3D** and **Square Landing** options.

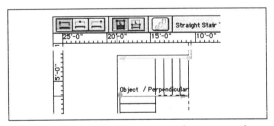

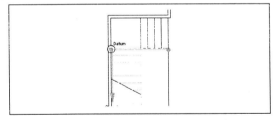

Starting from the designated corner, drag across a single flight-&-landing to meet the 3D stairs we produced at Ground level.

Then set Stair Preferences to **2D** and **Square Landing** only, and draw the two flights that will be visible from this floor.

(The first flight of stairs at Ground level will be hidden below the floor of the lower lefthand room)

To check that the 3D flights of stairs of the two levels meet each other as intended, view the Model in Left Isometric mode.

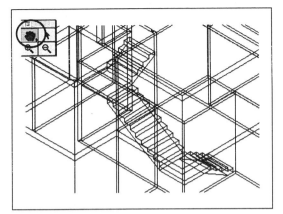

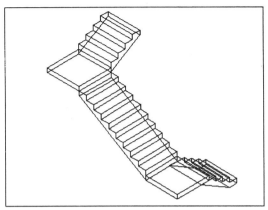

If the walls get in the way, simply double-click on our handy Hide Walls Command we made earlier. Click on the drawing once with the **Pan Tool** to force a redraw of the scene.

The result should look like this. If so, turn on the Walls again (else they will be invisible in all views in all layers). If not, check your procedure and/or fix it with **Moue 3D...**

On Movin' & Rulin'

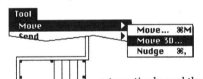

In situations where objects are misaligned for whatever reason and you need to fix it (e.g., when you change a layer's Z retroactively and the walls need moving up, or stairs are still being created from the old starting point), **Moue 3D...**—and its 2D counterpart, **Moue...**—are handy as they allow us to move objects with numerical precision instead of by hand. In the case of **Moue 3D...**, as we are moving by absolute coordinates, we can do so from any view (e.g. in plan to move something up or down in the z dimension).

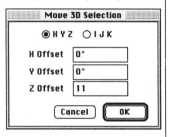

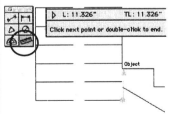

To establish how much an object needs to be moved, measure it first in a suitable view (in this case, Model layer, Left) with the **Ruler Tool** (Dimensions palette, **Windows : Tools** menu), which, unlike the standard dimensioning tools we'll see later, measures and give the result in the Data Display Bar without leaving a mark on the drawing.

Floors & Area Definitions

To help us in the design of the upper floor now that the stairs are in place, it would be a good idea at this point if we got around to defining the actual floor areas. Dealing as it does with the building as an integrated 3-dimensional entity, in MiniCad these are defined as actual slabs corresponding to the floor spaces in the real thing.

The first step is to define the footprint of the floor area. This is then extruded through Mini-Cad's special **Floor...** command to the required thickness.

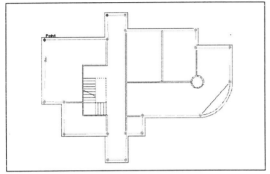

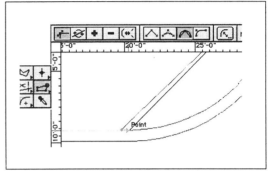

Starting with the Ground Floor level, draw a polygon along the inside faces of the external walls, using Snap to Object to click at the corners. Skip across any sections like the rounded wall which would entail working at much closer zoom: we will add them later.

Once completed, you can use the 2D Reshape Tool to amend any slight in inaccuracies which you may have made during the polygon's creation.

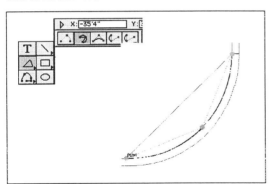

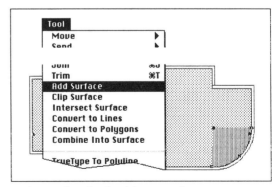

Use the Radial Arc Tool, Arc by Three Points mode, to create the arc area...

...then select both objects and **Add Surface** to combine into one.

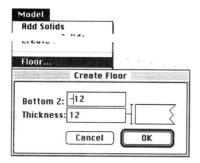

With the floor's footprint now ready, select it and choose **Floor...** (**Model** menu). You're presented with a simple dialog: how thick is the intended slab, and where does it start from. To ensure its top aligns with the foot of the walls, make these two figures equal, so that if the thickness is 12"[300], its **Bottom z** point is set the same amount below the layer's z, i.e. -12"[-300].

Floors: To Contain or Not to Contain?

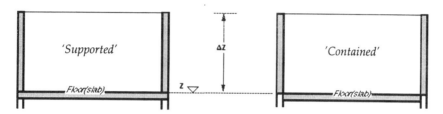

There are two schools of thought on whether in MiniCad floors should be drawn within the inside faces of the enveloping walls ('Contained'), or to their outer boundary ('Supported'). Which one you go for is largely a matter of personal choice, but you should be aware of the implications in terms of the structure of the file. I myself used to prefer the latter approach (above left) as it is a truer depiction of construction and (where such planning rules apply) returns a more accurate result in the calculating of areas. But it has two significant drawbacks:

a] the edge of the slab is then visible from the outside, and

b] it complicates the creation of walls underneath the floor: when walls are drawn, they automatically start at the layer's **z** and extend up to its full **Δz**. So a floor slab drawn to the outer boundaries will be inevitably be infringing on the tops of the walls in the layer below it (assuming it is set to start below the layer's **z**, to avoid trespassing on the walls on its own layer): unless, that is, those walls are lowered in height after their creation to accommodate the floorslab above or it is assigned its own layer.

Either way it is more work than we would really like. By the simple device of bounding the floorslab within the envelope's inner faces and dropping it below the layer's **z** by an amount equal to its thickness, the 'Contained' approach neatly sidesteps both problems. As for the area calculation problem, this can be solved by making a suitable amendment to formula used by the worksheet—as we will see later.

The result, when viewed in an elevational view such as **Front**, should look like this

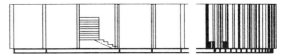

The floor slab is shown here with a thick line for demonstration purposes only. See box on previous page (Floors: To Contain or Not to Contain?) on the issues behind this approach

Since the Upper Floor has essentially the same footprint, it makes sense to copy it as the basis for its floorslab rather than repeating the same procedure in creating it from scratch.

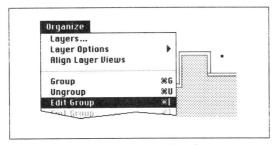

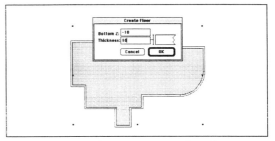

Fortunately, we can access this footprint—as with any Extruded object in MiniCad—by invoking **Edit Group** from the **Tool** menu. Do so, then **Copy** the footprint polygon, **Exit Group**,

then switch to the Upper Level and **Paste in Place** (Opt-⌘-V [Alt-Ctrl+V]). Then invoke **Floor...** again and this time make it 10"[250] thick with a **Bottom Z** of -10"[-250].

Of course we need to cut out the hole for the stairs. Not a problem: this, too, can be carried out on the 2D footprint at any time and it will be implemented in the 3D object, as with any Extruded object.

To make the appropriate 'cookie cutter' rectangle, we need to trace it off with reference to the stairs both here and on the Ground Floor. This calls for **Layer Options** to be set to **Show/Snap Others** (do that now), but also to be able to see through the footprint's fill pattern. To do that, we

go into Layers Setup, select our layer (**Upper Level**), then choose **Overlay** instead of the default **Paint** (=opaque) from the **Transfer Mode** pop-down menu. This makes the fill patterns of all objects in the layer translucent by making their Background pixels (the ones that are normally white) transparent.

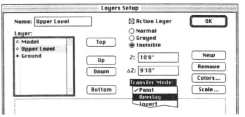

You might like to try out the other options in your spare time, but personally I've always found the first two to be the only ones I need.

Back in the drawing, create a Rectangle snapping to appropriate points of the stairs. **Copy** it, then **Edit Group** the floorslab and **Paste** it **in Place**. Give it a different fill pattern—the better to distinguish between the two—then, with both objects selected, call up **Clip Surface** from the **Tool** menu. The rectangle is the newer object and therefore in front and so it does

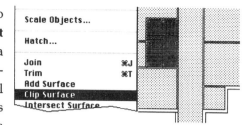

the Clipping. The screen should blink, confirming the action. Delete the rectangle to reveal the hole in footprint polygon, then **Exit Group** and change **Layer Options** to **Active Only** to see the result in the context of the rest of the drawing. **Save** your file.

Confirm the hole has 'taken' in the slab by viewing it in a 3D view like Right Isometric.

Note there is no fault line leading from one of the hole's corners to the perimeter of the slab. Had we simply **Extruded** *it, there would have been. Hence the importance of using the true* **Floor...** *option*

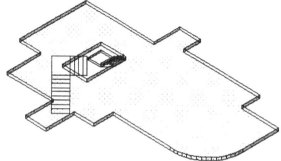

Now select the slab and choose **Edit Group** again.

Note that we don't need to be in **Top/Plan** *mode to snap back to a plan view of the footprint: a handy feature of the footprint editing facility.*

Like the proverbial factory that makes holes to put into Swiss cheese, the hole in the footprint can be edited just like the 'positive' part of the slab.

Of course, what's really happening is that you're still editing the 'positive' part – only from the inside.

Say, for example, we wanted to change the landing to an L-shape. This time, instead of creating a new cookie-cutter rectangle just so that we can **Clip Surface** again, let's use MiniCad's **Clip Tool** which allows us to take rectangular bites from any selected surface object in one go. You'll find it at the end of the 2D Reshape Tool's pop-out series: select it in its default mode (Remove area within the marquee etc.) and, using the upper right corner of the existing hole as our Datum, drag a marquee with it from 4' (610mm) down to a point Aligned with the width of the central axis as shown. Click to complete the Clipping.

A click on the 2D Reshape Tool would then reveal that the handles of the old hole are still in place, even though they are no longer needed. To delete them, we choose the 'minus' Mode of the Reshape Tool and click on each redundant vertex in turn.

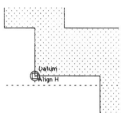

The Reshape Tool is helpful in other ways, too. Say—in anticipation of the need to deepen the rooms along the bottom of the plan—we wanted to extend just its lower half by 2ft [610mm].

 Mark the spot with the **Locus Tool** (alternative to the **Symbol Placement** Tool): use one of the bottom corners as a Datum, tab to the Y field and type -2' [-610] and Enter.

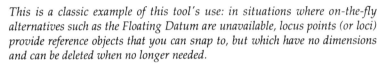

This is a classic example of this tool's use: in situations where on-the-fly alternatives such as the Floating Datum are unavailable, locus points (or loci) provide reference objects that you can snap to, but which have no dimensions and can be deleted when no longer needed.

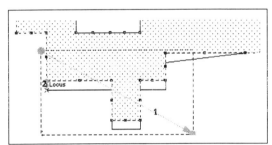
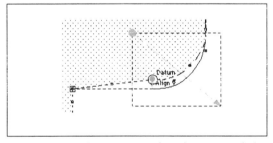

Then, click on the floor footprint with the 2D Reshape Tool in its default mode (Move handles of polygons), and click-drag-click a marquee around all the handles along the bottom up to but not including the curved wall. This tells MiniCad that you wish to move all these handles together in tandem. Drag the handle directly above the locus point down to snap to it, and click to set.

Now repeat the process for the area of the round corner. In this case, to ensure that you are dragging it down properly, as you drag bring the cursor first to the newly-moved corner it should aligned with, then with its current position, and click when you're Aligned with both.

Exit Group, snap the walls to their new positions as required, and repeat the procedure on the Ground Floor.

The Many (Other) Faces of the 2D Reshape Tool

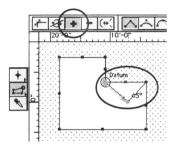

In addition to moving handles and eliminating vertices, the 2D Reshape Tool can also create new vertices through its '+' mode. This is done by simply clicking-&-dragging on an existing vertex (i.e. corner, as opposed to a handle in the middle of a segment).

Equally useful and perhaps more common is the tool's Change vertex Mode. This allows you to click on any vertex and change it from an angular corner to a spline curve of your choosing from the array of screenbutton options, namely:

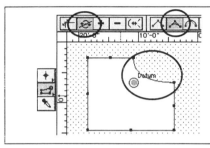

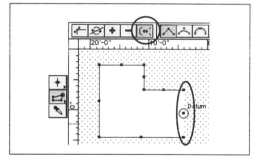

either a **Bézier** spline (describing a series of mathematical averages between pairs of points on opposite sides of the angle's sides)

… or a **Cubic** one (which runs the curve through the vertex in question)…

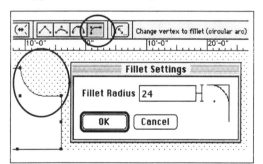

or a **Radial** arc which will make for the biggest possible radial curve that can fit in the given angle (unless you call up its Preferences dialog and give it a smaller radius of your choice).

The tool's final Mode is Hide/Show edges. This for situations where you wish to change a single or several specific edges of a polygon from visible to invisible or vice versa.

Defining Room Areas

Here's a nice trick to mark the completion of our basic plan layout and help us find our way around. In the Ground Floor layer, zoom in on the first room to the right of the top part of corridor. Make sure nothing is selected (double-click on a blank part of the drawing or on the Selection Tool itself in the palette) and choose a new default fill pattern, preferably one that is different to that of the floorslab.

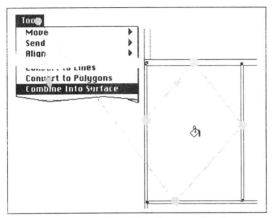

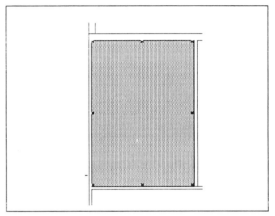

Now Shift-click on the four walls that surround it to select them, then choose **Combine into Surface (Tool** menu) The cursor turns into a bucket: click anywhere inside the room.

A new rectangle defining the area bounded within the walls should appear, with the new default fill-pattern.

The fill-pattern is merely to make it obvious that the object has been created.

Repeat the process with other rooms. As you can see, **Combine into Surface** is a great alternative to drawing polygonal areas manually.

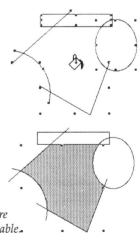

It works with any area that is fully enclosed within bounding objects: not just walls but lines, polygons, and even arcs. But it can occasionally be temperamental and require a couple of tries. Two conditions in particular must be strictly observed at all times:

a] The enclosure must be hermetically sealed: overlaps are fine, but the smallest gap anywhere and it won't work; and

b] No other object other than those directly bounding the area should be selected.

Which means that it won't work with the spaces surrounding the circular fireplace: the segments of a curved wall have slight gaps between them on the outside. It is also funny about walls that meet each other head on, as in the case of internal walls that are extensions of external ones. In such cases, manual drawing of the polygon is unavoidable.

On completion of each room area, name it.

In the MiniCad sense, that means selecting it, calling up its **Obj Info** palette, and clicking on the **Data** tab to view the user-defined information about it (which at the moment of course is still blank). It has a number of sections which we'll discuss later. For now, click in the first section at the top which is that of the object's Name and type the name of the space in each case.

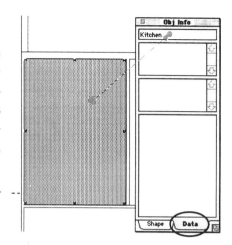

> *This information will come in handy later when we ask for automatic schedules to be made, so it's worth the effort.*

To ensure that we are referring about the same spaces, name them according to the following guide (the actual labelling on the drawing is optional).

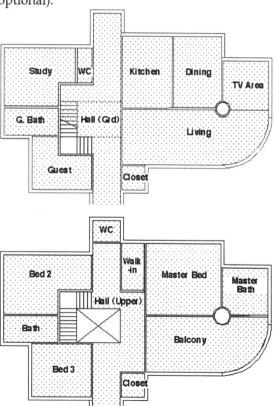

Ground Floor:

Upper Level:

When you're finished, **Save** your file.

Linear Dimensioning

At this point we have enough to go on to try out some of MiniCad's dimensioning features. These very straightforward and are accessed through their own **palette** from the **Windows : Tools** menu which we touched upon very briefly earlier when discussing the Ruler Tool.

Dimensioning of objects other than circles or angles is of two types: **Constrained** and **Unconstrained**. The difference between them is simple: the Unconstrained tool will allow you to measure on a diagonal, whereas the Constrained Linear tool will insist on measuring either the horizontal or vertical extent—i.e., the Δx or the Δy—of an object or collection of objects (the decision as to which depends on where you drag the cursor before clicking to set).

Unless your building is set at an angle on the drawing, your first port of call is most likely to be the Constrained Tool. It has one of five modes:

The first (the default) is the Constrained Linear Dimension, which is just your basic one-off measurement: you click on one point, click on the other, drag out where you want the figure and click to set.

> *As the points in question are usually snap points of objects, you will obviously have the Snap to Object constraint on.*

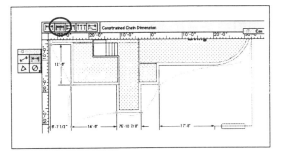

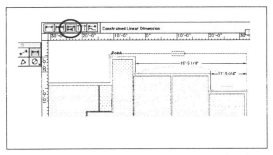

The second Mode is **Chain Dimensioning**: it starts the same way, but instead of dragging out and clicking the figure in each instance, it takes its cue from the first one and allows you simply to click on the other points which you want to measure to and it strings up the dimension figures for you along the same line.

The third option is **Baseline Dimensioning**, which is applied in exactly the same way but results in the dimension figures being offset progressively further out and measuring distances from the starting point.

The fourth Mode is **Ordinate Dimensioning** which is typically used to mark off heights in elevations or distances from a given datum.

The fifth Mode—**Selected Object(s) Dimensioning**—is a handy shortcut in situations where you only need to measure the overall (horizontal or vertical) extent of a selected object or Group of selected objects: just click to set.

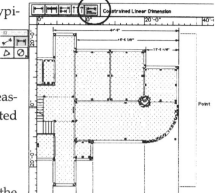

Unconstrained Dimensioning works along exactly the same lines but features only the first three Modes of its Constrained counterpart.

Editing Dimensions After the Event

Dimensions, like walls, are Groups of a special kind (a 'high-level object', in MiniCad's parlance). Unlike standard text which you might write with the Text tool, you can get information about them and edit them through the Object Info palette in much the same way as you would any graphic object. This comes in very handy when one wants to change just one or two dimensions without changing the defaults. Select one or more of the dimensions you put down and press ⌘ I [Ctrl+I] and see for yourself.

Virtually all aspects of the dimension can be viewed and changed from their default settings, including:

- the Dimension Standard used
- whether witness lines should be present or not
- whether the arrows (if applicable) should be inside or not
- attributes of the text (font, style, size—although these can be changed through the file's standard **Text** menu)
- whether it (they) should be Primary or Secondary
- the preferred precision display
- whether the text should be set within a box
- whether the dimension value should be displayed at all
- any unit marks or abbreviations should be displayed before (Leader) or after (Trailer) the figure
- the required Tolerance (Single, Double, Limit or None)

Classes: An Introduction

With the drawing fairly cluttered now with dimensions and room area objects, the question arises: how can we remove them without actually deleting them from the drawing? In traditional CAD systems the solution would be to assign them to separate layers of their own and turn these off, but consider: with dimensions and room area objects needed for every level, that would mean we would need three times

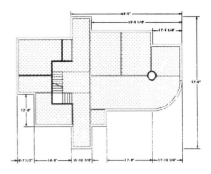

as many layers as we have at the moment. And that's just the start: we would have to do the same for the usual aspects of construction, e.g. Sanitary, F&F, M&E, Furniture, etc. Which means that for a building of *m* number of storeys and *n* number of aspects, we would need $m \bullet n$ number of layers to give us the flexibility to produce the various layout permutations we need. That's a lot of layers, and a lot of turning on and off—as a glance at any typical AutoCad working drawing will confirm.

MiniCad avoids this proliferation by a simple line of reasoning: since we're unlikely to ask for a drawing which shows two floors with, say, the M&E on one and not on the other, why not create a second means of structuring the file, so that each aspect of the building can be assigned its own category which can be turned on or off across all Layers at any one time, and use these in combination with the Layers setup to create any combination of drawing that we want?

Classes are just this sort of category. A simple example of how they work is with the dimensions we've just made. MiniCad as a rule is thankfully free of assumptions about how we work, but since it is a fair bet that we will want to dimension things at some point and get these dimensions out of the way at times, it creates two default Classes in every file: **Dimensions**, and

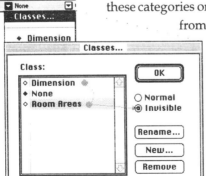

a neutral one called **None** for everything else. The dialog where we can turn these categories on or off as well as make new ones of our own is accessed from the **Classes...** pop-down in the Data Display Bar.

Also from the **Organize** *menu—but that's a trek.*

Do this now and, in the dialog, select the **Dimensions** class and click the **Invisible** button on the right. The hollow diamond confirms its new status.

Unlike Layers, Classes cannot be Grayed— possibly because it would make for too many permutations what with the **Gray Others** *Layer Options, as well.*

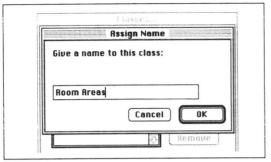

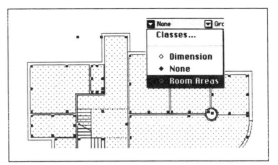

Before returning to the drawing, click on the **New...** button and name this new Class **Room Areas**. Then **OK** this dialog and mark it **Invisible**, too, before **OK**'ing the main dialog.

The dimensions have duly disappeared, but the room area objects haven't because they don't know yet that they should belong to the new (invisible) Class we've just made. Assign them now by Shift-selecting them and then choosing **Room Areas** from the Class pop-down.

*An important advantage over Layers: no **Cut**-&-**Paste** is involved*

The plan should once again show pristine walls.

*Remember: these 'disappeared' items haven't been deleted, and can be brought back at any time by marking their Class **Normal** again.*

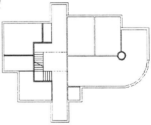

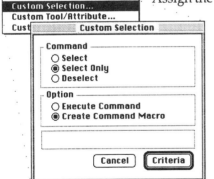

Assign the room area objects on the Upper Level, too. Only this time, instead of Shift-selecting them, use the **Custom Selection...** shortcut, based on a common feature which is unique to them.

It works just like its sister **Custom Visibility...** :

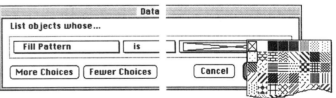

In this case choose **Select Only**, make it a Command Macro if you like...

and the Database Criteria dialog, choose **Fill Pattern** from the list, then select the one you used for the objects, and **OK**.

Symbols

General

At this point, it would be a good idea to put in some doors and windows. As objects that repeat themselves throughout a drawing, these are classic examples of MiniCad's **Symbol** facility, which is expressly designed to make the duplication and editing of recurring graphic objects easier and more economical with system memory.

> *That's **RAM**—Random Access Memory, akin to remembering to 'carry 1' or whatever when doing sums—not to be confused with **hard disk space**, which is long-term memory, if you like. Although that, too, benefits, since using symbols results in smaller file sizes.*

So symbols are basically duplicates, but of a special kind: they can be placed on the drawing with a single click precisely where you want them, and they are universally linked to their original prototype in such a way that changes made to any one are reflected in all the others as well. They have many other advantages, too, which we shall appreciate as go along and which will hopefully persuade you of their preference over simple duplicates.

But the symbol 'status' should not be reserved only for objects that repeat themselves many times in a particular file. Any item that is likely to be needed in other drawings should be considered (because symbols can be pulled in from other files without leaving the file you're working in). In addition, walls in MiniCad require that any item intended to be inserted properly in them—e.g., doors and windows—must be made into a symbol first, even if only one is required.

The creation of a new symbol means that the prototype is stored away in the file's symbol library (part of its **Resources**): thereafter **instances** of it are placed in the drawing, as often as we like.

Symbols may be 2D only, or 'hybrid' 2D/3D, which means they may be a fairly complex object in the 3D model but have a simplified appearance for drafting purposes in the working drawing (**Top/Plan**)—or vice versa. (In the absence of a specially-designed 2D aspect, 3D-only symbols, appear in the working drawing as they would in **Top** View). This independence between the two aspects or components of a symbol gives considerable freedom and flexibility.

As symbols that are placed in walls, doors and windows are slightly special cases, because the walls, being hybrid 2D/3D entities themselves, place certain restrictions on their handling, as we will see later . However, we will start with them as they are logically the next thing for us to do, and because the other types will then seem that much easier.

Windows

In drawing the prototype/master of a window, it is easier —though not essential—to do so in the context of the wall for which it is intended.

 I would also strongly advise—although this is undocumented—that it is oriented horizontally. For some reason instances of symbols that were created with a vertical orientation don't behave well when it comes to inserting them in walls.

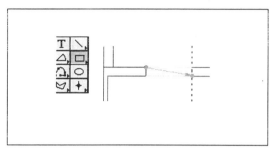

Marquee-zoom in on any section of a horizontal external wall. With the default fill-pattern set to Solid, white color, and both Snap to Edge and Smart Points constraints on, make a 4' [1200mm] rectangle for the opening of the thickness of the wall.

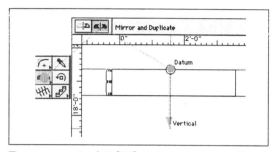

Draw a nominal 2" [50] rectangular frame from the left, then duplicate it on the right by choosing the **Mirror Tool** in its Mirror and Duplicate Mode and dragging an imaginary axis straight down from the opening's Center (press Shift to ensure it's vertical).

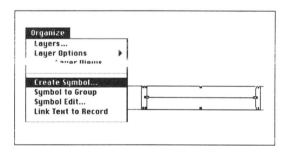

With the basic prototype now ready, draw a marquee around the whole caboodle to select it all and choose **Create Symbol...** (**Organize** menu).

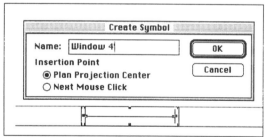

In its dialog, call it, say, **Window 48 [Window 1200]**, and **OK** it with its default **Plan Projection Center** insertion point.

Wall symbols are always snapped to the centerline of the wall, so the fact that it will be placed by its center point in this case suits us fine.

The prototype then disappears, because it's been taken to become part of the file's Resources.

To introduce instances of it back in the drawing, we double-click on the **2D Symbol Insertion** Tool (or press ⌘ R [Ctrl+R]). This calls up the Resources palette which we dismissed at the very start of the file when it was still meaningless to us.

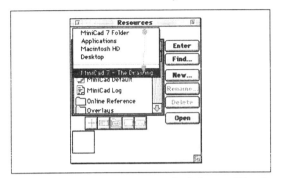

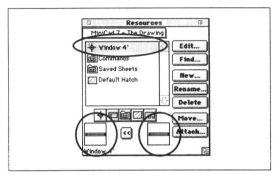

You won't see our new symbol there. That's because by default MiniCad always takes you to its own folder. To access the Resources of our file, click-&-hold on the little pop-down at the top and drag down to our current file listed at the bottom, below the separator line.

And there's the new symbol, at the top of our file's Resources. The little white square on the bottom right shows us what it looks like; the one of the left shows which is the current active symbol. They should be the same.

Not because it is the only symbol so far, but because a symbol that has just been created is always the new active one.

Anatomy of a Resources Palette

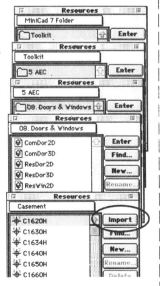

The list above the separator line in the pop-down illustrated above describes the filepath to the MiniCad 7 Folder. You go down the list to go 'up' the hierarchy of files on your hard disk in your search for Resources in other files, and double-click on a folder in the main window to go down it, one level at a time. The Toolkit folder that came with your application, for example, has many interesting Resources you might like to explore: as you drill down the folders that interest you, you ultimately see not folders but 'dog-eared' icons with cubes on them: these are MiniCad files.

A double-click on one of these accesses its Resources: any of these can be **Import**ed to become part of your current file; if it's a symbol, you can also **Select** it to make the new active symbol—(an action which effectively Imports it, too).

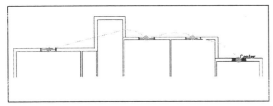

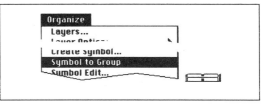

With that in mind, place a few instances by doing quick clicks with the Symbol Tool at the Centers of the sections of the Study, Kitchen, Dining & TV rooms walls.

> *MiniCad knows where these points are thanks to the proper junctions with the internal walls defining each of these rooms. This allows us to insert the instances from a greater zoom-out that would otherwise be possible.*

We can use this symbol also as a basis for a new one—say, of a different size.

> *This method of making new symbols is often easier and quicker than making it from scratch.*

To do so, we place an instance of the first one in a blank part of the drawing, then 'de-symbolize' it by demoting it, from **Symbol to Group** (**Organize** menu).

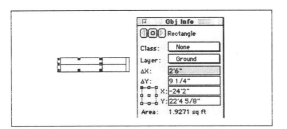

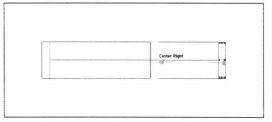

As an ordinary Group, we can now **Edit** it in the usual way (⌘ [[Ctrl+[] is the shortcut). Select the opening rectangle and, through its Obj Info palette, reduce its Δx to 2'6 [750].

Then drag across the right jamb by its Center Right handle to snap to the Center Right of the new opening, and resize the glazing line to end at the Center Left handle of the right jamb in its new position. Then **Exit Group**, **Create Symbol**, etc.

Know Thy Cursors

This is as good a point as any to rehearse the distinction between two important types of cursor:

- You *move* a selected object(s) with the **Snap Drag** cursor: a 'Crusader cross' which appears when the cursor is near (but not directly over!) a selected object's handle. That handle becomes the 'anchor' by which the object (or collection of objects) is moved, so you can snap with it to a desired point.

- To *resize* a selected object(s) you bring the cursor directly above the handle, and the cursor changes to a **Resize** cursor, showing two arrows pulling in opposite directions.

> *The cursor changes to other forms in other contexts, but these are the two important ones.*

Editing Symbols

Distribute instances of both windows—and any others which you might like to make—around the plan on both layers. Then check in either layer in an Isometric view: as you can see, they don't register as yet in the 3D model. That's because these symbols have only a 2D (drafting) component. To appear in the 3D model, they must be given a 3D aspect. This is an editing task, which is done via the Resources palette.

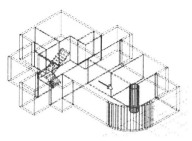

 Usually, a symbol can be accessed for editing purposes by simply selecting any of its instances then choosing **Edit Symbol** *in the* **Organize** *menu (where* **Edit Group** *normally appears). But this: a] accesses its 2D component only, and b] doesn't work with symbols placed in walls: select one and the whole wall segment in which it resides gets selected, too... Walls are very proprietorial toward their symbols, like a mother bear toward her cubs.*

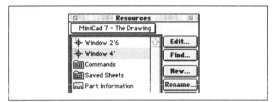

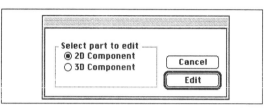

Within the palette, select the symbol we wish to work on—say, the Window 4' we created first—then click on the **Edit** button.

It asks us which part of the symbol we want to edit. As a general introduction, and to have something to work from, stay with the (default) **2D Component** for now, and **Edit**

Just as in **Edit Group**, the rest of the drawing disappears and an **Exit** button appears on the upper right. Unlike **Edit Group**, however, an x and a y axis run through the center of the object: their intersection marks the symbol's Placement Point. We can the position of the object in relation to that point if we like, or any other aspect of its appearance, and, upon **Exit**ing, the effect would be apparent in all instances of it in the drawing.

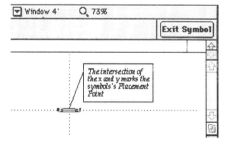

For now, though, just **Copy** what you see here to use a reference when creating the 3D component. Since there is no 'Switch to 3D component' button or command, we need to **Exit** and then repeat the procedure of Editing, this time choosing the **3D Component** option.

> *Actually, you can skip the* **Exit Symbol** *button altogether and just go straight to* **Edit** *button in the Resource palette...*

The 3D Edit Symbol environment looks much the same as the 2D one. The difference here is that we are in fact viewing the symbol in **Top**, not **Top/Plan**, view. Since the 'action' of the symbol's 3D component takes place in elevation—i.e., the fact that it has a frame that starts at a particular height above the ground and extends up a certain height etc.—we should switch to a **Front** view. Its third dimension—its depth—will be taken care of by simply Extruding the frame details.

This is the guiding rule in deciding in which view to create any 3D object: the starting projection is the one in which the profile is the most intricate and cannot be easily created through Extrude, Sweep or Multiple Extrude—more of which later.

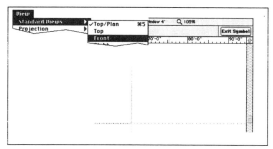

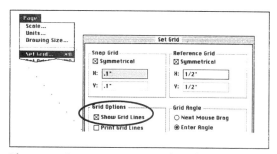

You should be able to see the symbol's ground plane (which will align itself with the wall's starting **Z**) as a horizontal line.

If not, go into **Set Grid...** and make sure **Show Grid** is on.

Now **Paste in Place** the copy of the 2D details we made earlier. They will assume the same coordinates in this x-z view as they did in the x-y view of the 2D component: that is to say, sit astride the ground plane. Using their Center Left handle as our Datum and Snap to Object and Smart Points constraints on, use tab-and-type to start a rectangle for the window opening at a height of your choice, e.g. 3'3 [1000]. Make its Δx=4' [1200] and drag it up, say, a ΔY of 44" [1120]. And click to set.

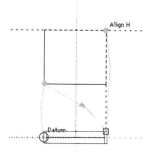

To achieve its purpose of cutting a hole in the wall (this being the structural opening), this rectangle must have no fill in it. So, while it is selected, make sure its fill in the Attributes palette is set to None.

Alternatively, you could **Convert** *it* **to Lines** *(Tool menu), which would remove any fill since it will no longer be a surface object. But that would also create four objects instead of the one, which is why I prefer the other method.*

Now we must Extrude it: if we don't, it will remain a 2D object, and MiniCad is ruthless in this respect: any 2D object left behind when gets 'dumped' immediately in the symbol's 2D component the moment you Exit the 3D component, leading to surprising and unintended results in the working drawing. For the same reason—and since they're no longer needed— delete the 2D plan objects we Pasted in by way of reference.

We've Extruded before, so there's no mystery here. With the rectangle selected, press the Option [Alt] key to get **Extrude...**, and type the thickness of the wall: 9.25 [230], and **OK**.

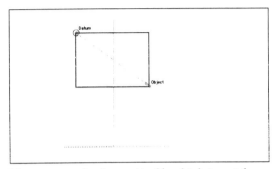

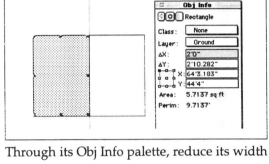

Now create the frame itself, which is cut from a rectangle of the same size. To make it easier to see what we're doing, give it a fill pattern.

Through its Obj Info palette, reduce its width to half its current size.

We can't do this manually, because 3D objects don't have snap points along their centers.

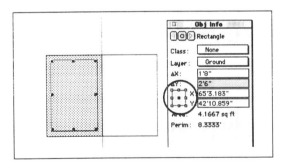

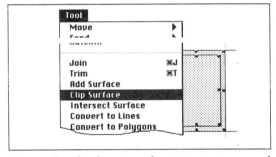

To cut out the glazed area, duplicate it on the spot by clicking on it with the Option [Alt] key. To shrink it in relation to its center 2" on all sides for the frame, click (while it is still selected) on the central selection handle in its Obj Info palette, and reduce both its ΔX and ΔY by 4" each.

Then select both rectangles, **Clip Surface**, and remove the inside rectangle. The resulting frame can be Extruded if you like, but if you don't need that degree of realism a more RAM-efficient policy would be to leave it flat.

That is also the case with the sample window symbols provided in the Toolkit.

The effect of mullions can be created simply by drawing lines across the glazed area.

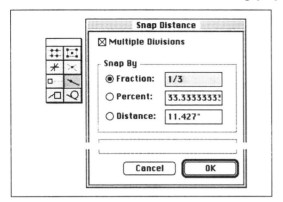

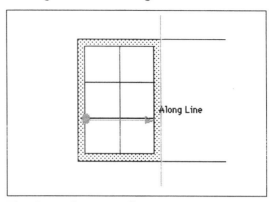

To help us get the proportions right, double-click on the Snap to Distance constraint to get its dialog. Type **1/3** in its **Fraction** field, & **OK**.

The SmartCursor will now snap to 1/3 distance along the inside of the frame, making the horizontal mullions easy to locate.

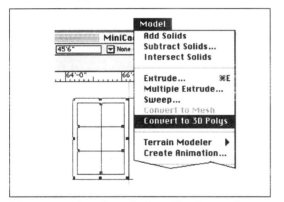

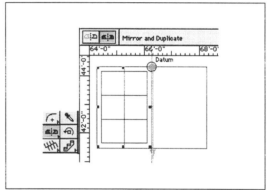

Marquee-select the whole collection and **Convert to 3D Polys** to make them bona fide 3D objects, albeit flat ones.

Mirror-&-Duplicate the result before switching to **Top** view (*not* **Top/Plan**) to make the final adjustments to the object in terms of its placement in the wall in plan.

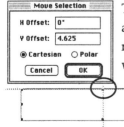

The 3D window objects we created—opening, frame, mullions—were created on the same default plane: this is the (x-z) plane of the symbol's Placement Point (*see circled*). If we want the 3D symbol to sit in the center of the wall, we need it to sit astride this plane equally on either side. This means moving the structural opening object up by half the wall's thickness. We do so using **Move...** (**Tool** menu).

And that's it. **Exit Symbol** and view the model in an Isometric view.

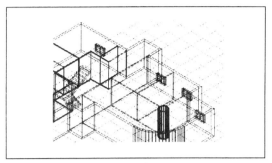

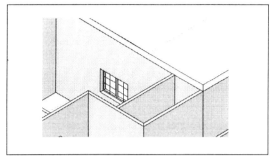

You should see the windows now.

Rendering the scene **Shaded Solid** will confirm that the holes have taken.

The process of making the 3D component must be repeated for each master symbol, as that information is lost during the **Symbol to Group** procedure. But there is a work-around: **Paste** a instance of the symbol to be varied in a new MiniCad file. Edit its 2D and 3D component as required, then **Rename** it through the Resources palette. Then **Import** it into your original drawing.

◊

Doors

Door symbols operate on very similar principles and provide good practice of the general procedure at this point. The difference is mainly that in the 3D model we may see the door ajar — i.e., have objects projecting outside the wall—and that in the working drawing the impression must be given of a complete break in the wall.

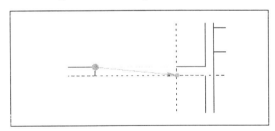

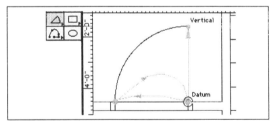

Zoom in on a horizontal piece of internal wall and draw a rectangle for the opening — say, 3' (900mm) wide, and the depth of the wall (4"/ 100mm).

Make the usual frame of 2" [50mm] on either side, then use the Radial Arc tool in its default mode to draw the door swing (touching the startpoint midway to activate Align), then a line for the door leaf.

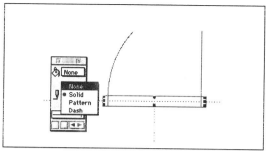

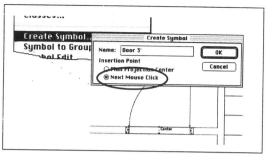

For the appearance of a break in the wall, select the opening rectangle, and set its fill and its Pen (boundary line) to None, i.e. invisible.

Why not simply delete it completely? Because we will need its Center snap-point later.

Marquee-select the collection and **Create Symbol...**. Only this time, make the Placement Point not the default **Plan Projection Center** but **Next Mouse Click**, & **OK**. Back in the drawing, click at the Center of the structural opening

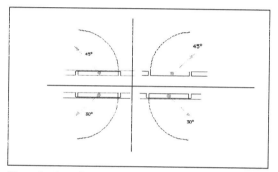

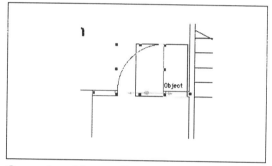

Test placing the new symbol in the same wall— but this time *hold when you click* and move the cursor in various directions away from the placement point. 'Ghost' arcs appear, so you can decide which to go for—right- or left-swing, in or out— before committing yourself.

Once placed in a wall, you can slide a door or any other symbol along it to a required position—although in most cases you will use the Floating Datum for accurate placement, taking into account half the symbol's width since it is placed by the center of its opening.

By touching with the Symbol Placement cursor on a snap point that you wish to align to, you can take advantage of the SmartCursor to place instances in precise relationship to existing objects on the drawing.

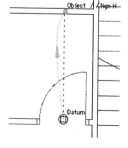

The procedure for making variations on the same door is similar to that of windows or any other symbol: take a new instance (not placed in a wall), **Symbol to Group** it, **Edit Group** as required, then **Create Symbol...** again.

The procedure for making the door's 3D component is also similar to windows.

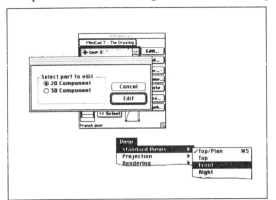

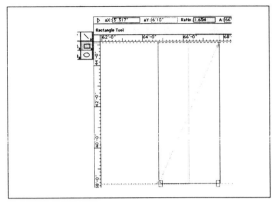

Select the door master symbol in the Resource palette, click **Edit...**, **Copy** its 2D component for a moment then go to its 3D component, switch to **Front** view, **Paste in Place**, and draw up the rectangle for the structural opening. Set its fill to None, **Extrude...** it to the thickness of the wall,

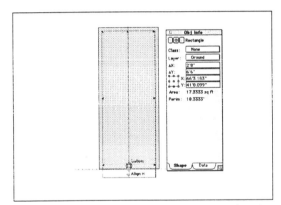

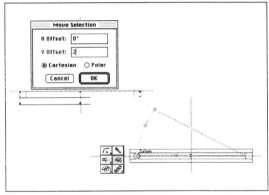

draw new rectangle of the same size for the frame, then duplicate and reduce that to create the cutting rectangle. This time, however, as the frame is to have no bottom section, enlarge the cutting rectangle to go beyond the frame's bottom edge, and then **Clip Surface** with the two selected. Delete the cutting rectangle, and **Extrude** the frame profile by the desired thickness. Then draw a rectangle for the door leaf, and **Extrude** that, too, if you can spare the RAM…

—or better, simply use **Convert to 3D Polys** to make it a flat 3D object. Then switch to **Top** view, **Move...** up the structural opening and frame to straddle the creation plane (corresponding to the wall's centerline).

As a final touch, if you like, select the door leaf and, with the **Rotate Tool**, swing it out by its hinge.

Check your handiwork in an Isometric view.

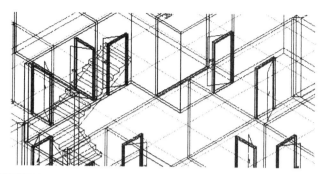

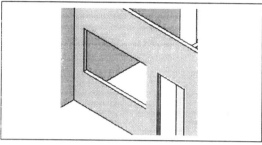

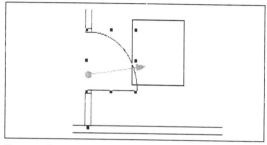

Remember, a wall symbol can be simply a hole— as in the wall of the breakfast counter or the serving hatch between the kitchen and dining room.

> *There is another way to make a hole in a wall, using the new* **Subtract Solids...** *facility—but more of that later.*

Remember, too, the right procedure for deleting wall-based symbols: *pull it out of the wall first* before deleting it—else you'll delete the wall itself, too.

◊

Duplicate Symbols in Wall & Other Pointers

On occasions when you want to place a series of the same symbol in a stretch of wall—say, a set of regularly spaced windows or a range of patio doors—individual click-and-placing can be a little tedious. Since ordinary duplicate facilities (⌘ D/Ctrl+D, etc.) are not available to wall-based symbols (selecting the symbol selects the wall, as well, remember) MiniCad has a special **Duplicate Symbol in Walls** facility.

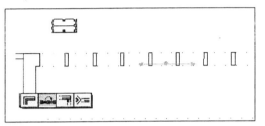

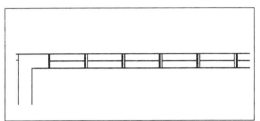

It is applied using a tool in the Wall Tool series. Selecting an instance of the required symbol anywhere in the drawing (not in the wall itself), you click-&-slide the cursor back and forth on the target wall to reveal ghostlines of duplicates distributed along it, at a varying distance that you can change in this way before clicking to set.

The result—as many duplicates as can fit within the section at the distance you specified—appears on release of the mouse.

In situations where you want numerical control over the operation, you can use the tool's dialog, called up by clicking on its Preferences button in the Mode Bar:

The first field relates to the distance of (the placement point of) the first instance in the series from the end of the wall segment. The second field is the distance between each instance, and **Copies** is…–er, the number of copies.

The box at the bottom explains each of these as you move the cursor over them.

Note that you can opt for manual control for any of these parameters by use of the mouse.

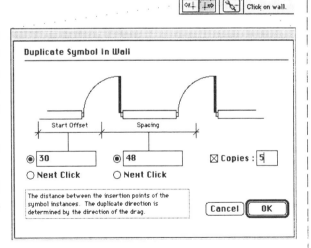

Other Symbols

Under this category come all the non-wall-based symbols, and these are much more straight-forward in terms of the constraints on moving, placing and duplicating them. This is a good point to explore, through the Resource palette, the libraries provided in the application's Toolkit folder, and Import them into our file, and then use to 'populate' our house with the various fixtures and fittings, sanitary, furniture and other objects of your choosing.

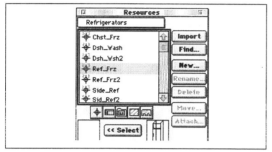

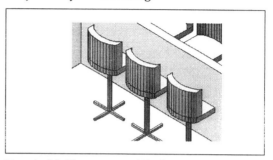

Note the small 2 and/or 3 next to each symbol icon, indicating whether it has a 3D component. Remember that whereas a 2D-only symbol will not show up in the 3D model, a 3D-only symbol will appear in the working drawing as seen in its **Top** view until such time as a 2D component is made for it.

Be mindful how many 3D objects you place in the file. They may look good in the Isometrics but they add quickly to the RAM memory requirements. You might find the best idea is to make them 2D-only (by **Symbol to Group**ing them, then making them new symbols), changing to their hybrid equivalents later on for presentation purposes (see later, **Symbol Edit...**)

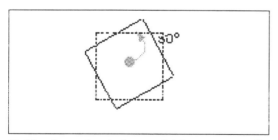

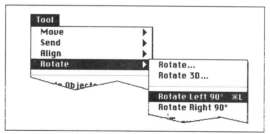

Unlike doors & windows which automatically take on the orientation of the wall, freestanding symbols land on the drawing the way they were made, so if you want them at a different angle you need to click-and-rotate before you release the mouse button.

Alternatively, you can place them first and then **Rotate** them: either by a specific angle (in the **Rotate...** dialog, or—if it's a 90° job—use the ready-made **Rotate Left** or **-Right 90°**

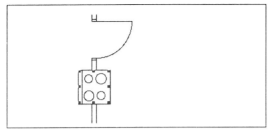

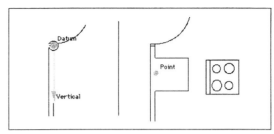

You'll need to watch out when placing symbols next to walls: they tend to get 'sucked in'. The only solution to this is either to place them well away and then move them… —

—or create a temporary 'distraction' by drawing a line or any other object covering the wall face. This provides a kind of 'shield' during which symbols can be placed on the wall face with impunity. The line can then be removed.

This is particularly crucial with items such as electrical switches

Organizing Your Symbols

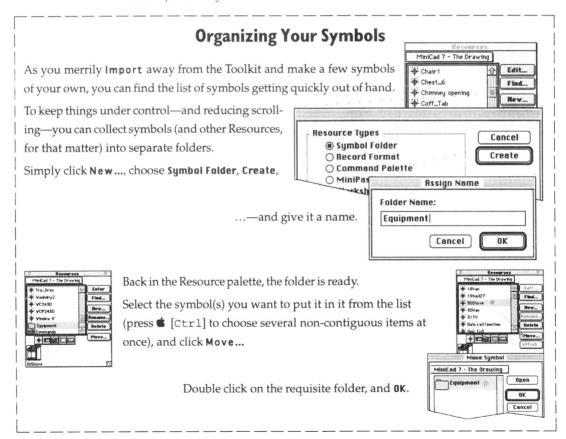

As you merrily **Import** away from the Toolkit and make a few symbols of your own, you can find the list of symbols getting quickly out of hand.

To keep things under control—and reducing scrolling—you can collect symbols (and other Resources, for that matter) into separate folders.

Simply click **New…**, choose **Symbol Folder**, **Create**,

…—and give it a name.

Back in the Resource palette, the folder is ready.

Select the symbol(s) you want to put it in it from the list (press ⌘ [Ctrl] to choose several non-contiguous items at once), and click **Move…**

Double click on the requisite folder, and **OK**.

x

Updating Stationery Files

You may remember I mentioned at the start of the book that as we go along we can and should update our Stationery file to reflect the additions that we make as go along. Well, now is an excellent point to demonstrate how this is done.

Remember that a Stationery file is meant to provide us with a file that is blank and Untitled but with our favorite settings already in place. At the beginning, this meant only things like Units, Scale and Drawing Size, but by now we have quite a few more features to add, such as layers, symbols, and classes.

The principle is simple enough: we delete from the file anything that is specific to this particular project and not likely to be called for in others:

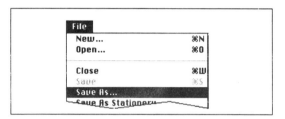

But before we do, **Save** it **As...** (**File** menu) a different name : e.g, **Stationery.temp** [temp.sta]

This is to avoid inadvertently changing our current file.

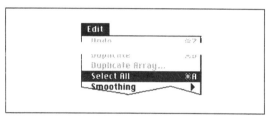

Proceeding from layer to layer, **Select All** (⌘ A [Ctrl+A] and delete to ensure they are empty.

The keyboard shortcut for going to the next layer: press ⌘[Ctrl] and the up or down cursor, as required.

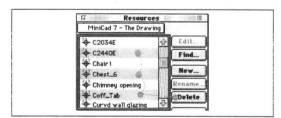

In the Resource palette, select and **Delete** the symbols that you think you won't need in other projects.

Remember the ⌘[Ctrl] key for making non-contiguous selections.

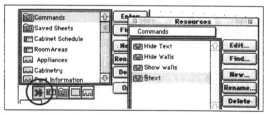

Turn off the long list of symbols by clicking on the symbol button below it, and double-click the Commands item to access the ones we made earlier, and do the same there.

This is also, of course, the way you would access the list to edit it under normal circumstances.

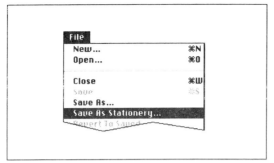

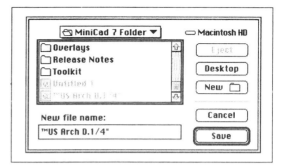

Applying the same principle to other Resources such Saved Sheets and to the Class Setup, we are now ready to **Save As Stationery...**

To make sure you are replacing the old Stationery with this newfangled one, choose precisely the same filename and folder, and **OK** the subsequent dialog asking you confirm.

◊

Roofs

As with floors and stairs, MiniCad automates the task of making pitched roofs. The procedure is similar to that of floors: first you draw the roof as it would appear in plan, then you invoke the **Roof...** command (**Model** menu) and tell it what angle, miter, etc. This is done for each facet of the roof separately.

As a somewhat Modernist building, the project we've made so far is not really a good candidate for roofs of this type, so instead we will take advantage of our updated Stationery file to quickly create a new design more suited for the purpose. This will also help us review what we've learned so far.

Open our revised Stationery file either from within the program or from the desktop. In the Ground Floor layer, after checking that the Wall Preferences are set to $9\,^1/_4$" [250mm], start from point A and use the familiar tab-and-type input method to create a footprint of the following dimensions:

*Note that section **D E** is created by entering an L of the figure shown, and an A(ngle) of -45°.*

In the Upper Floor layer, with **Layer Options** set to **Show/Snap Others**, trace over the walls of main section Add windows as appropriate.

(The space at the bottom left is a garage)

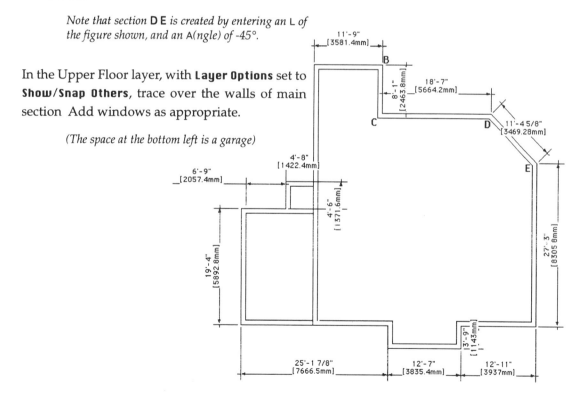

Since they usually occupy a distinct zone of their own, roofs are usually placed in a layer of their own, so that the calculations as to their starting **Z** etc. are made easier. But not always: our first example—that of the roof over the garage—we will in fact create in the Upper Floor layer, since its starting height coincides with the top of the ground floor walls. With that layer still active and **Layer Options** set to **Show/Snap Others**…

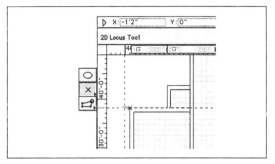

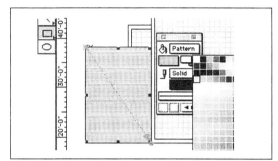

Zoom in on the garage and place two locus points: one on the corner of the structure, and the second the required eave depth – say, 14" [350mm] from that corner, aligned with the outside face of its rear wall.

Then draw a rectangle from it to the corner of the main structure.

I suggest using a vertical line fill and, if you like, with the Background color (the default white rectangle) made a desired shade of slate or tile.

Patterns that use a light line or dots against a dark background are often more effective than their dark-on-light equivalents

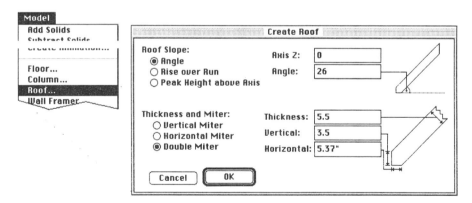

With the rectangle still selected, choose **Roof…** (**Model** menu), and in its dialog enter an **Angle** of 26° (**Axis Z**—the height of its support on the wall—stays zero for now). Choose the **Double Miter** option and enter a **Thickness** of **5.5**" [**140**], a **Vertical** of **3.5**" [**90**] and whatever **Horizontal** results. And **OK**…

ARCHITECTURAL DRAFTING IN MiniCAD 7

Back in the drawing, the program waits for you to indicate the line where the roof is supported on the wall—its **Axis line** (*see next page*). Click-*drag* (no dainty click-clicks here…) this imaginary line from the first locus down the outside face of the side wall .

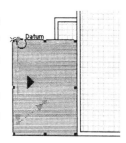

An arrow head will appear, pointing right or left as your cursor moves across the page. It's asking you to indicate which way lies the ridge of the roof. Make it point to the right, and click.

Before checking the result in one of the 3D views, let's quickly make the gable end. This is done by simply drawing a wall at the appropriate position, then reshaping it to fit in the appropriate elevational view.

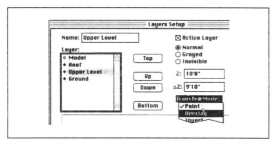

In order to see where to draw the wall, go into the **Layers...** dialog and set the **Transfer Mode** of this (Upper Floor) layer to **Overlay**.

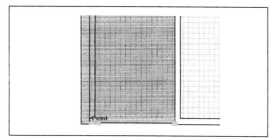

Draw the wall…

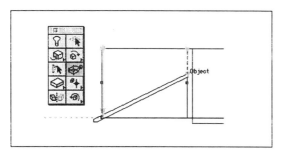

–and switch to a **Front** view. Click on the 3D Reshape Tool: the wall's handles change from two at the center of either end to one at each corner. Drag down first one, then the other top corner to just below the roof element. Use the Object snap-point as your guide.

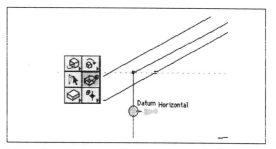

Note that if the wall's length needs fixing, it can only be done by dragging one of the original center handles, so you will need to do this first before dragging the corner handle into place. If necessary, reveal the center handle by dragging the corner back up or down first.

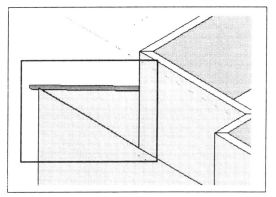

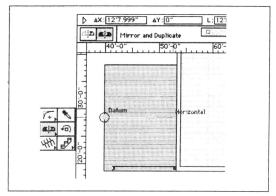

Now check your handiwork in **Right Isometric**. If it passes muster, press ⌘5 [Ctrl+5] to return to **Top/Plan** view…

–and Mirror-Duplicate it to the other end with the axis of reflection being the horizontal middle of the garage wall.

About (Roof) Axis Lines

The concept of the **Axis Line** of roofs is inextricably bound up with that of the **Roof Plane**. Each is understood in terms of the other.

Basically, a pitched roof's Axis Line is where the rafters sit on the supporting structure. Simple enough, except that this 'sitting point' is not necessarily the underside of the rafters, but rather wherever the roof's 'roof plane' is defined. And this varies in MiniCad according to the type of miter used:

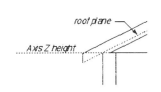

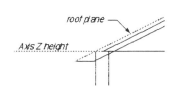

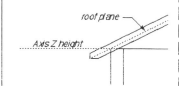

If vertical, the roof plane is the underside of the rafters.

If horizontal, it's their top surface.

If double (as in our case), it runs through the miter point.

Since the result determines how high or low the roof sits on the wall, the choice of miter used is particularly important when deciding the **Axis Z** height in the **Roof...** dialog.

Hips, Intersections & Dormers

The main roof works along the same principles, although here, as we said, a special layer *is* recommended, which most likely also incorporates the ceiling of the upper floor, if applicable.

With the Upper Floorplan as our current active layer, click on **New** to create this layer with the correct starting **Z** automatically entered, and with the same **ΔZ** (although it could be made smaller—having no levels above it, it really doesn't matter).

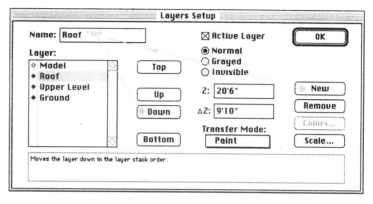

A simple gable roof is achieved in much the same way as for the shed/garage: you create one half, then Mirror-Duplicate it to make the other. But when hips and valleys, intersections and dormers are involved, the first step—much as in traditional drafting—is to work out in advance the basic roof plan we're after. First, in the Upper Level, use the Polygon tool to square off the upper right corner to serve as a balcony), then in the new Roof layer, with **Layer Options** set to **Show/Snap Others**,

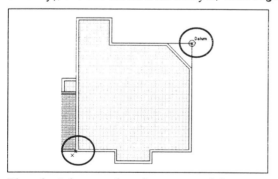

Place loci there and at the corner of the main structure near the garage, and another at the outside corner of the triangular balcony at the back. Continuing the eaves theme of earlier, place additional loci at offsets of 14"(350mm)— along both x and y axes—from the first two.

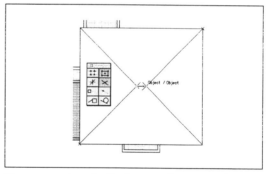

Draw a rectangle that snaps between them— preferably with a white fill—then single lines from the corners towards the center, constrained to 45° (press Shift) until they overlap. Then with Snap to Intersection on, draw another line to represent the short ridge that forms between the hip intersections.

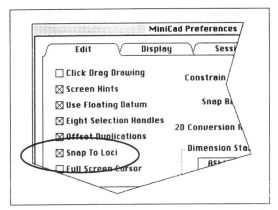

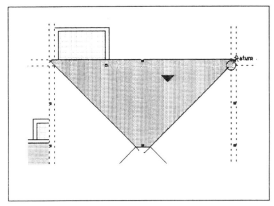

Since the rectangle obscures the structure corners, to enable us to see where to draw the Axis lines, go into **MiniCad Preferences...** (**File** menu) and turn on **Snap to Loci.**

Draw the polygon of the first section, invoke **Roof... and** draw its Axis line along the inner snap line.

In view of the bigger spans, though, make larger **Thickness** *and* **Vertical** *settings*

On Picking Up & Putting Down Attributes

Emulating the particular combination of Foreground and Background colors used in an object drawn earlier is a typical application of the **Eyedropper Tool**. As its name and icons suggest, it is used to copy attributes such as fill patterns, color of pen or fill, line weight etc. from one object to another in one operation.

In its default mode, the Eyedropper is in 'Pick up' mode, symbolized by the eyedropper.

The 'Put down' mode (icon: upturned bucket) is of course used on the target object. Note that it can be invoked by simply press-and-holding the Option [Alt] key, so you never actually have to click on it in the Mode Bar.

The precise set of attributes you wish to apply is determined in the tool's dialog which is called up by its Preferences button the Mode Bar.

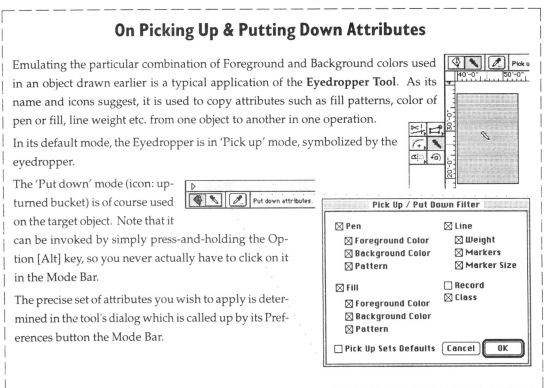

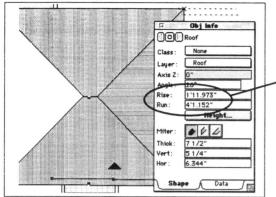

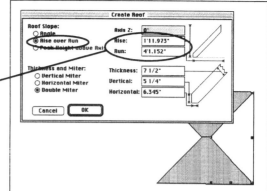

Mirror Duplicate that section using the ridge as the axis, then draw the polygyon of one of the side sections. Before **Roof...**-ing it, though, select one of the previous ones and note the Rise and Run figures.

To ensure that it meets the existing sections properly, in the new section's **Roof...** dialog choose the option of **Rise over Run** rather than **Angle**, and verify that those figures are the same as those of the others.

While there, check that the other settings such as Thickness, Vertical, and Miter type also tally.

Now check the result in an Isometric view. While you're here, you may as well select and delete the 2D elements, as they're no longer needed. Assuming it's OK, return to **Top/Plan** and Mirror Duplicate the new section across the Center of the ridge.

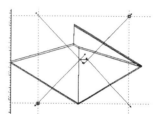

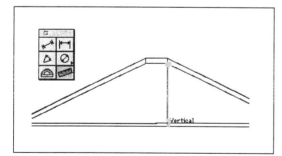

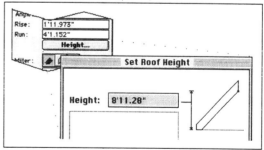

In situations where it is not OK, you can always correct the new section's pitch manually by measuring the height that it should be to its underside in an elevational view…

—and entering that figure in the **Height** field through its Obj Info palette.

Intersections & dormers

The roofs of the front portico and the rear annex are instructive in the principles of intersections and dormers. In each case we apply the **Roof...** routine to a polygon describing one half of the desired addition/dormer in plan. The guiding rule is simple:

> *Provided the angle of the valley line is 45°, the same parameters that applied to the main roof can be used to create a matching valley line in the new addition.*

With this in mind, and starting from a locus point at the same offset as before from one corner of the front...

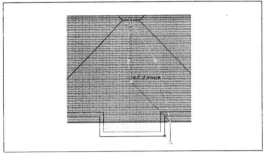

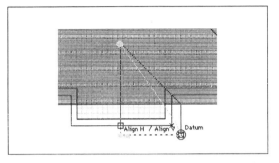

draw a polygon that meets the main roof line perpendicularly then goes up at 45° until it aligns with the center of the ridge.

On completion, **Cut** it to memory (⌘ x [Ctrl+x]), then select the main roof section and ⌘ [[Ctrl+[]) to Edit its 2D 'footprint'.

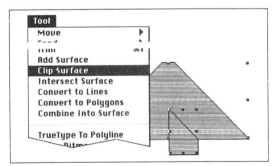

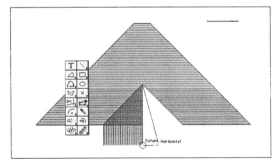

Paste in Place the remembered polygon, and use it to **Clip Surface** the main roof polygon. Then Mirror it (without duplication)...

...–along the intended ridge and use the 2D Reshape Tool to pull its bottom right handle away from the section already cut before applying **Clip Surface**. Then **Exit** the footprint.

Clipping objects that align exactly with one or more of the target's sides tends to confuse the program and can result in the whole of the target object disappearing.

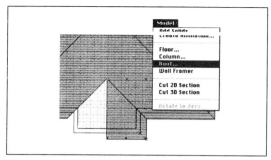

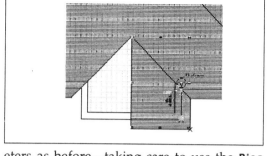

The main roof section is now cut, ready to receive the new addition. **Paste in Place** the polygon again (it should still be in memory). Apply the **Roof...** routine with the same parameters as before—taking care to use the **Rise over Run** mode— and draw the Axis line along the external wall as before, oriented of course towards the center.

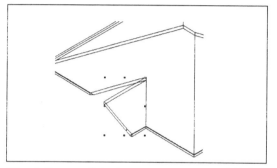

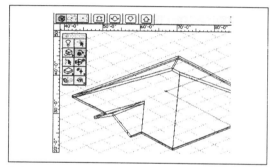

Check the result in **Right Isometric**, and if OK, return to **Top/Plan** and mirror-duplicate it across its ridge.

Select any one of the roof sections and, with the **Flyover Tool** in its first mode, click-and-drag to inspect the result from all angles click-and-drag the model this way and that.

This is one of my favorite tools, although by rights a better name for it would be 'Craftsman's Bench' or 'Pedestal'. I prefer the first mode (Rotate about the center of selected object(s)), as the other two are about rotating around the horizontal or vertical planes, and are less intuitive

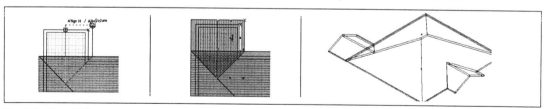

Back in Roof Plan, zoom in on the rear projection and repeat the process there, preferably starting from the section away from the edge, checking the results from the various angles as before.

Assuming all is well, we create the gable ends in the same way as before.

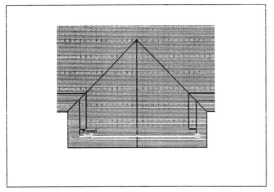

Draw the wall, snapping to the one in the layer below

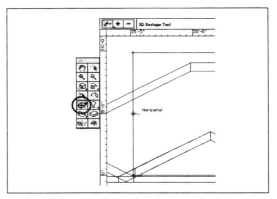

With the 3D Reshape Tool in default (resize) mode, reduce the width as required

Remember the central handles are required for this operation, so it must be done first

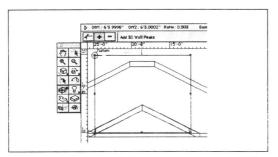

With the same tool in Add 3D Wall Peaks mode, click-drag a peak vertex to the wall

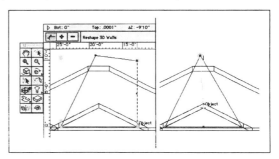

Then back in its default mode, drag down each of the top vertices to their bottom counterparts.

F i n a l l y,
switch to the Model layer and link
it with the Roof layer (since we haven't
done that yet),
and check the result in **Lower Right Isometric**.
Repeat for the annex gable.

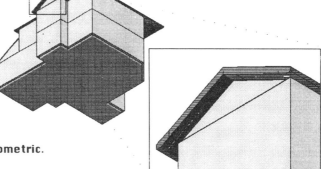

Detail Work (2D)

Layers for Scale

Having completed the basic fabric of the building, the rest is largely to do with features such as front portico, columns, internal and external balustrades etc. If you are concerned with purely 2D drafting, this involves the straightforward application of circles, lines, rectangles etc. For a 3D model, however, such items must also have 3D components, the heights of which can only be determined through parallel development of a notional section through the building. Either way, we are led naturally to an another very important application of layers, namely for scale.

MiniCad's approach in this matter is different from that of traditional CAD applications. Instead of carrying out everything at 1:1 ('world scale'), with the required presentation scale set only for specific output, each layer can have its own scale, which is that at which it is also printed. This means that one layer can be set, say, to 1/8" [1:100], and another at 1:1/2 [1:25], and the two shown together so that a detail and a general arrangement drawing can be shown apparently side by side. At the same time, all objects remain true to their intended size and can be dimensioned at all times for a correct readout.

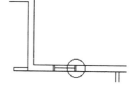

To illustrate this, return to the Ground Plan and draw a no-fill circle around one of the window jambs, such as you might use to highlight a detail. Then **Copy** it to memory (⌘ C [Ctrl+C]), and

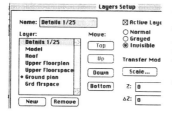

go into the Layers Setup dialog. Click **New**, zero its **Z** and **ΔZ** settings (it will play no part in the 3D model), give it an appropriate name, and click on the **Scale...** button. This gives us access to the same dialog we encountered at the beginning of the file. Choose **1:1/2 [1:25]** and **OK**.

The fact that we haven't done so till now tells you that a new layer always takes on the scale of the active one unless otherwise specified

Back in the Layers Setup, make sure our new layer is the new Active one, and that only the Ground Floor layer is **Normal**, and **OK**.

Set **Layer Options** to **Show Others** to reveal the Ground Floor plan, and **Paste** (⌘ V [Ctrl+V]) the circle in memory in our new layer. Note that it is four times as large as its twin is in the Ground Floor—reflecting the difference between the two scales—giving ample scope to draw the detail, while enabling us still to enter true sizes in creating the components.

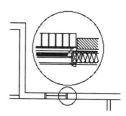

The 'Jotting Pad' file

Earlier on, we saw how a sketch model of a scheme can seamlessly be converted to working drawings, with the details added in afterwards. The development of these details and how they relate to each other wasn't discussed, but in fact it, too, can and should be carried out within the program. Due to the experience of complicated, menu-driven and line-based programs, we tend to think that the 'D' in 'CAD' stands for 'drafting' only; but thanks to its 2D-3D facility, the immediacy of its tools, its accuracy and its versatility with 2D surface areas and (in v7) of 3D volumes, MiniCad makes a great sketchpad and should be regarded as an integral part of the *design* process, too, no less than the old pencil and paper.

Because these 'sketches' involve the ad-hoc creation of experimental symbols and other Resources that can get in the way of the actual project file, though, I find that it is a good idea to do your on-screen doodling in a separate MiniCad file (either completely **New** —⌘N [Ctrl+N]—or launched from standard Stationery) to run in parallel with the main file.

I call it the 'Jotting Pad' file or whatever, and it is particularly handy in establishing the heights and **Z** attributes. Knowing it is a separate file allows you to be less precious when fashioning details, creating unfinished symbols or redundant Classes or layers, and generally to test ideas without fear of impacting on the actual job at hand. In this way one may combine the advantages of rough-and-ready sketching with the confidence that comes with knowing that the results are dimensionally accurate.

A typical example is the notional section seen here—really a composite through various parts of the building—of our second scheme, and I recommend this technique in your own work.

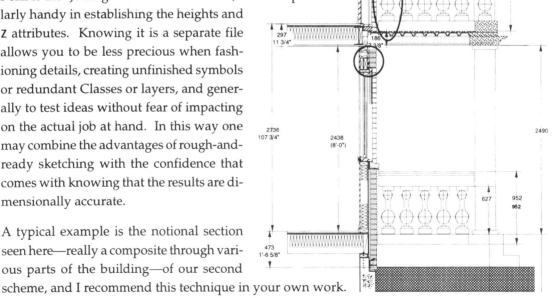

It is at this point that one also gets to use some other tools and tricks of the program.

Hatching

You may have noticed that fill patterns stay the same absolute size regardless how far you zoom in or out. This is fine in some cases, but hopeless when it comes to brick elevations and other cases where the spacing needs to be true to the scale being used. This is where true **Hatches** come in, which are composed of true lines that are drawn in for you by the program to fit the required area.

A typical example is the hatching of the brick sections. Since many are involved and they will no doubt be needed in other jobs, it makes sense to create a symbol of each brick type or size, such as the one in our example. The procedure is simple: draw a rectangle 3-5/8" by 2-1/4" and keep it selected.

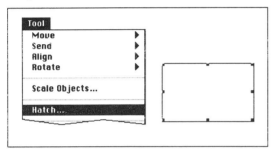

Choose **Hatch...** (**Tool** menu).

This menu item is only enabled when a polygon or other surface-type object is selected

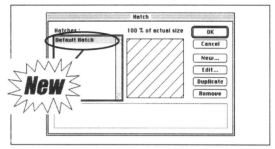

A default hatch pattern is provided, along with any others you may have Imported earlier (they being Resources like symbols). If you haven't,

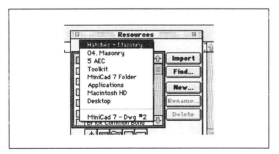

why not make one now: there's a Brick (Section) hatch in the Masonry folder of the MiniCad Toolkit, as well as a few others which will come in handy, such as Concrete & Concrete Block

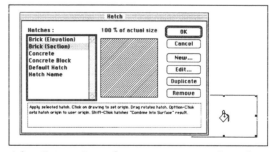

After Importing, choose **Hatch...** again, select the **Brick (Section)** one from the list, then **OK** and click inside the selected rectangle.

Note the hints given when you hover with the cursor over the OK button.

The result can be a little confusing, because although the lines duly appear, one sees no selection handles (which should, after all, be there). This is an illusion: the handles of the polygon and of the Group of lines which is the hatch pattern are cancelling each other out, because they precisely overlap.

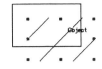

So if you don't like the result and want to delete the lines, make sure you click somewhere first to deselect both, then click on one of the lines to select the hatch by itself.

 The Hatching operation is also sensitive to the scale of the active layer: at scales such as 1/8" [1:100] the lines may be too far apart. For best results, use in layers set to detail-type scales, e.g. 1:1/2" [1:25], 1:1" [1:10], etc.

If you don't find the one you need and like a challenge, you can always **Edit...** an existing hatch or make a **New...** one of your own in the Edit Hatch dialog:

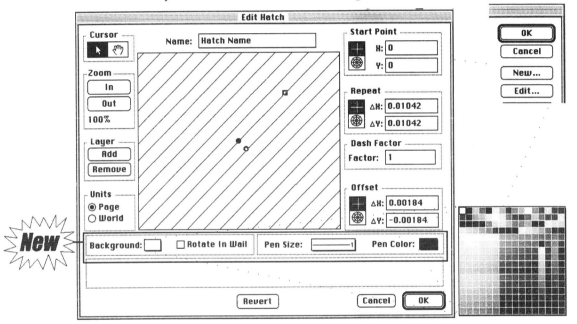

The Edit Hatch dialog offers a wealth of options, including composing the hatch of more than one 'layer' (each one of which has lines going in different directions), orienting the lines by hand or numerically, <u>setting special colors to the background and/or the lines</u>, and—a very significant improvement—<u>the option of having the lines rotate in line with the angle of the wall</u>, where applicable.

Knock yourself out.

Radial Arcs (other Modes)

 Mortar joints demonstrate the use of radial arcs by other modes: specifically the rather nifty Arc by Two points and Center, which allows you to manipulate by eye the desired center, after clicking on two points representing the arc ends. Although they are tiny, it makes sense to make a symbol for them, since they repeat at every joint to create as many duplicates as required at the appropriate offsets (Option-⌘-D [Alt-Ctrl+D]).

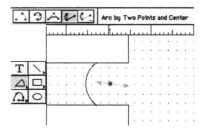

 Insulation, by the way, is another good candidate for symbolizing, the repeating graphic being the bit which fits inside an imaginary rectangle, comprising two lines and three radial arcs (*see box, next page*).

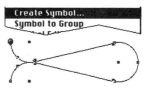

Dimensioning Angles

Accessed through the Dimensioning tools palette (hotkey: ',' [comma]), this has two Modes:

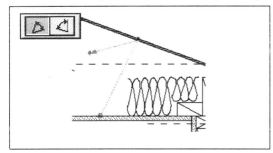

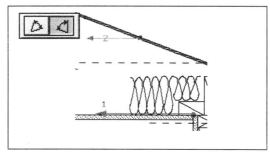

Angle between two objects (default), where you click on one side of the angle (a line or even a polygon side), then on the other, and pull out to place the dimension figure, and…

Angle between reference line and object, where you click-drag an axis line (often, but not necessarily, orthogonal), then click on the line or polygon side whose angle in relation to it you wish to measure, pull out and click to place.

Center Mark Tool

 An stablemate of the Diameter Dimensioning Tool in the Dimensioning tools palette, this places a center mark on selected circles, and rounded corners of rounded rectangles, with a single click. Umpteen uses.

Off on a Tangent...

The insulation symbol is a good example of the **Tangent Constraint** being applied:

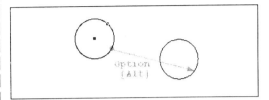

Make a circle of any diameter (we'll resize it later to suit), and Option [Alt]-drag a duplicate away to one side.

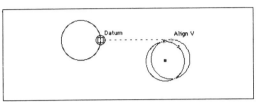

With the Snap-Drag cursor move the duplicate till to Align its Top Center with one of the Center points of the original

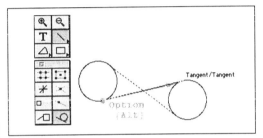

With the Tangent Constraint on only, click on the left circle and press Option [Alt] to switch to the opposite Tangent as shown. Draw to the other circle till Tangent there, too, is confirmed.

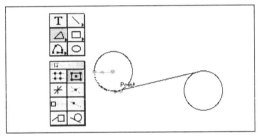

Turn *off* Tangent Constraint (it would get in the way), turn on Snap to Object, and draw a Radial Arc (default mode) from 9 o'clock to the end-Point of the Tangent line (*not* the circle's Bottom Center)

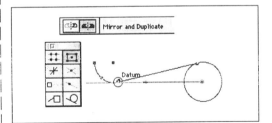

Delete that circle and Mirror-Duplicate the tangent and arc across the axis from the second circle's Center

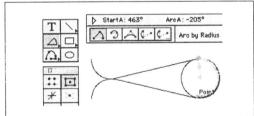

Draw the arc of the second circle from Point to Point of the two tangent lines. **Group** and resize as required via the Obj Info palette. **Create Symbol...**, with one of the free arc ends as Placement Point.

Structural Shapes

If I've resisted the impulse to switch to the **AEC Overlay** (**File** menu: **Overlays**) till now, it's because the **7.x Standard** [ZSTANDRD] **Overlay** provides all the functionality we have needed so far. More to the point, it includes one menu item that has unaccountably been omitted from the **AEC Overlay**, but which is nevertheless indispensable, to my mind, namely **Structural Shapes...** (**Tool** menu).

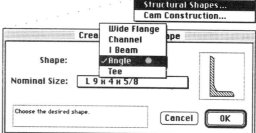

It features a simple and very straightforward dialog, giving access to ready-made I-beams, channels, angles, etc. in a wide range of nominal sizes. The resulting profile is an ordinary 2D polygon that can be resized, extruded or otherwise edited as required. A great timesaver.

See Appendix on how to use the Overlay Edit utility to add this menu item to the AEC Overlay and generally customize the MiniCad interface to your requirements

◊

3D Details

Sweeping

MiniCad's facilities for creating custom 3D objects (i.e., other than walls, floors and roofs) are fairly versatile, and having established the relevant heights, Z positions etc. that apply, one should have all the requisite information to hand.

The next step is to consider carefully the level of detail actually needed. Even with the use of symbols, too many or overly-detailed 3D objects dramatically raises the RAM memory overheads and processing time of the file, making it virtually impractical to view even a modest project such as ours at anything other than wireframe.

A trade-off is called for. One approach is to consider the MiniCad model as a conceptual one, to be exported at this or a later stage to a dedicated model/rendering package such as, *Strata Studio Pro, Infini-D, Art*lantis* etc. for greater detail to be added and for high-level rendering for presentations. The other is to create two Classes of 3D objects: one High Detail, for use only in restricted contexts showing part of the building at a time, and the other Normal (or just the default **None**) for use the rest of the time, to give just enough an impression of the final result.

A good example is balustrades. Ideally, it would comprise repeated instances of a baluster symbol, created from a lovingly fashioned profile (using the polygon or polyline tool in **Front** view) and…

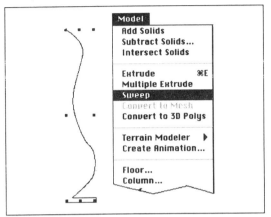

…**Swept**ed (**Model** menu—pardon my grammar). The result is an object in which the number of segments is determined…

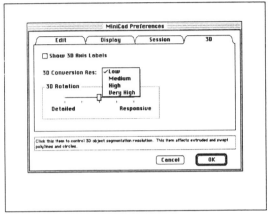

…— by the **3D Conversion Resolution** setting in **MiniCad Preferences**. The default **Low** is equal to 16 segments in a full circle

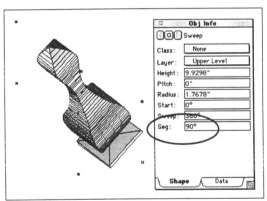

The precise number of segments can be controlled subsequently through the object's Obj Info palette: simply work out the angle that each segment would have, type it in, and Enter. 90° is good enough for most purposes.

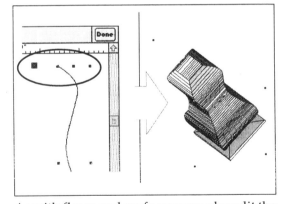

As with floors and roofs, you can also edit the object's profile at any time by the usual **Edit Group** routine. Placing a (single) locus point in the profile redefines the sweep axis to be somewhere other than the profile's startpoint.

Remember that another powerful factor at your command is the ability to vary the size of the sweep angle: it defaults to 360°:

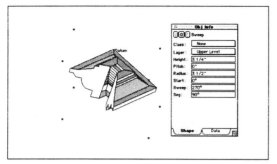 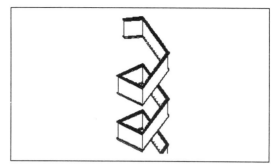

but it can be less...   or indeed more, to create a helix.

The helix effect is achieved by ensuring that the Pitch—*i.e., the height that the sweep achieves after one full circle—is higher than the* Height *of the profile itself. Using a suitable profile, a segment size of 90° and a locus placed at the center of a square stairway, even bannisters can be created.*

Other things to bear in mind: if you create your Swept object while in **Top/Plan** mode, the result will be an object lying on its side, with the default 'ground plane' of the layer running through its center. For the object to stand upright—such as a light fitting—you need to swing it into position within one of the elevational views after creating it in **Top/Plan**.

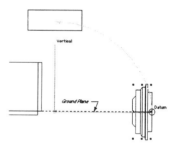

Note that the 2D Rotate tool is perfectly suitable for this purpose

Alternatively, create it within one of those views to begin with.

Columns

Columns, too, used to be created by Sweeping — mainly because Extruding a circle would result in the number of sides changing every time the **3D Convert Res.** figure was changed in Preferences — but in v7 a special routine has been devised that allows columns to be created in plan from their footprint, just like **Floors.** Sweeping is still necessary for complex bases & capitals, but for the shaft itself, the procedure is now as simple as it can be: Select your footprint, invoke **Column...** (**Model** menu)

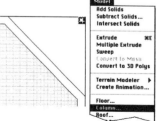

And type in the height you require in the dialog.

Multiple Extrude

After Extrude and Sweep, this is the third main method for creating objects other than the architectural staples of floors, roofs and columns.

In contrast to Sweep which swivels the same cross section around an axis, **Multiple Extrude** (**Model** menu) allows you to assemble the object from a series of profiles along its length. These don't have to be, but in practice usually are, of similar shape or at least follow some kind of evolutionary logic. The order of the sections in the object reflects that of the 'pile': this is usually the order in which they were drawn (last drawn = frontmost = top), unless it was modified afterwards through the use of one or more of the **Send** options (**Forward/to Front/Backward/ to Back — Tool** menu).

In the right context and with some planning, Multiple Extrude can be a powerful tool: the offsets between the sections are admittedly always equal (see below), but as we shall see later this is easily modified subsequently. You could conceivably use it to create certain kinds of column capitals, but a better and less ambitious example of its use in an architectural scenario is the creation of ramps of complex profiles:

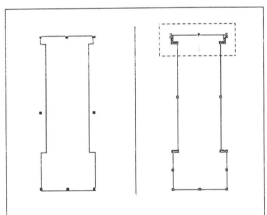

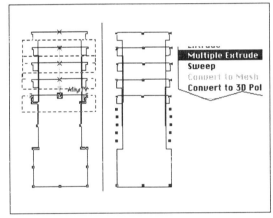

Working in **Front** view, fashion the profile of the ramp at its highest point as a single polygon, duplicate it without offset, then with the Reshape Tool in its default mode draw a marquee around *all* the vertices of the coping and drag that down by its Top Center to maintain its integrity while shortening the midsection*

Repeat the duplicate-and-shorten procedure three or four more times.

A series of locus points duplicated at equal offsets to ensure a uniform slope is a good idea

Finish off by duplicating the shortest profile on itself, then delete the locus points (very important!), select all and **Multiple Extrude (3D)**.

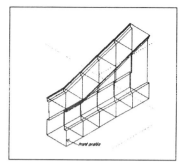

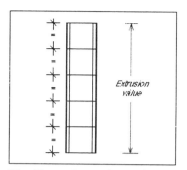

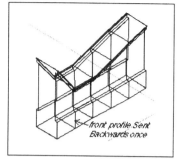

A Right Isometric shows clearly the order in which the sections were created…

The Extrusion value refers to the whole of the object, with the sections being equal parts thereof

…this, like the profiles themselves, can be changed at any time through the normal editing **Enter Group** procedure

Add Solids, Subtract Solids, Intersect Solids

These commands are three facets of a new feature in MiniCad 7. Fulfilling the same function in 3D that Add Surface, Clip Surface and Intersect Surface do for 2D, they complete the line-up of MiniCad's creation tools for custom 3D objects. For industrial designers and architects of the Frank Gehry school of design they are no doubt a godsend. In more standard architectural practice the need is possibly less acute, but it is nonetheless useful wherever the other methods fall short. Since these tend to be features that are highly project-specific, I leave it to you to find suitable examples in your own work. The procedure, however, is very simple, and a good example of its application in standard design is in the cutting out of holes in walls which would otherwise entail making a one-off wall symbol (as we saw earlier with the breakfast counter).

Say, for example, in our first project we wanted to place a serving hatch between the kitchen and dining room.

To establish the width of the required hole in a way that can be seen in one of the elevational views, we would mark the points with the **3D Locus Tool**

2D loci would not be viewable in such views

We would then to switch to the appropriate elevation view: in this case, **Right**

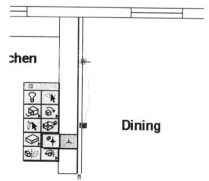

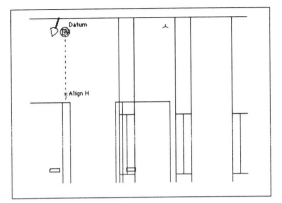

Start a rectangle in alignment with one locus

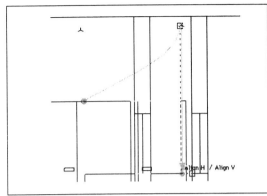

and finishing with the other

The precise positioning of the rectangle-cutout is important, because unlike a symbol it won't be easily moveable afterwards.

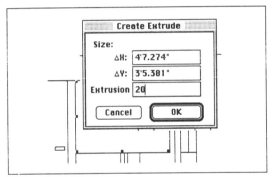

Extrude... the result by a thickness noticeably thicker than the wall

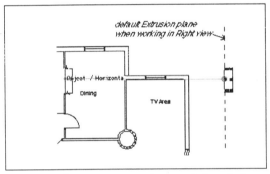

then switch to **Top/Plan** view and drag it from the default plane where it was created & extruded to the wall in question

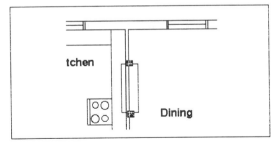

Manoeuver the box into position and delete the loci which are no longer needed, switch to

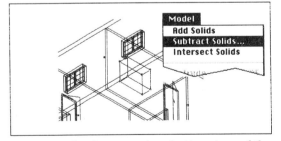

an Isometric view to gain a better view of the proceedings, Shift-select both box & wall and invoke **Subtract Solids...**

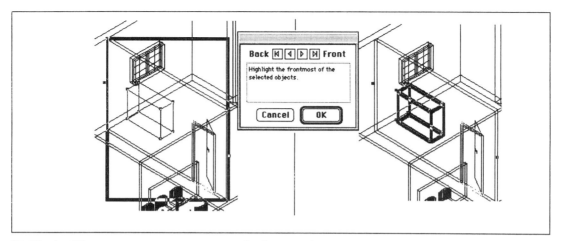

Unlike its 2D counterpart **Clip Surface** which immediately uses the frontmost object to cut the other, the Subtract Solids dialog asks you which of the objects is to be subtracted from by clicking on the **Back** or **Front** button, highlighting each in turn.

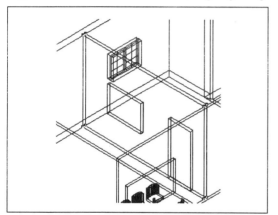

The result in wireframe...

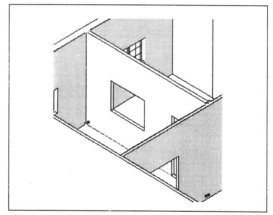

...- can be confirmed when Rendered.

The routine is will not work on walls that have had extra vertices add to them, such as gable ends — even if these vertices are subsequently removed.

Add Solids... and **Intersect Solids...** work on the same principle, only without the need for a dialog.

3D Sections

Before the days of **Subtract Solids...** (i.e., in previous versions), there was only one to slice away from 3D objects, and that was **Cut 3D Section** (**Model** menu). It's less needed now, but it still comes in handy for sectional elevations or other cutaways for design or presentation purposes. It is also good for situations where **Subtract Solids...** won't work, such as 3D objects that are no longer considered Solids because they have been **Convert**ed **to Mesh** or to **3D Polygons (Model** menu), or a Linked Model, where—because it is a reflection of what is going on in other layers—the objects are **Lock**ed, i.e. not changeable. To demonstrate:

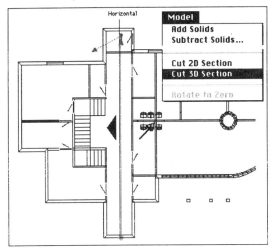 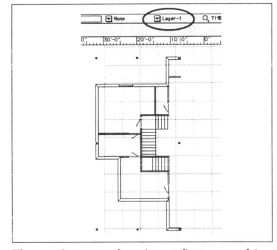

Switch to the Model layer, **Top/Plan** view, call up **Cut 3D Section**, and click-drag down an axis of your choice—say, the main hall. A fat arrowhead appears, similar to when creating a roof: it is asking which part do you want kept. Drag to the left and click.

The result seems alarming at first: everything behind the line has disappeared, as if deleted. Never fear: the action has been carried out on a *duplicate* which has been placed in a new Layer of its own, which by default is called Layer-1

Being a duplicate, this can be viewed, manipulated, and edited to your heart's content without affecting the original model. Bear in mind, however, that a new Layer is created with every **Cut 3D Section** operation, leading to a proliferation that you may not want. Which is why I tend to carry out my 3D Sectioning in a separate file into which I've Copied and Pasted the relevant items.

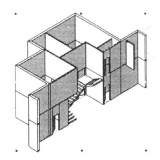

2D Sections

Cut 2D Section works the same way as its 3D counterpart: you click-drag the section line, and click again to indicate the direction of view. Since section drawings are an intended part of the project file anyway, and because they usually involve the whole or significant parts of the building which cannot easily be copied and pasted into other files, this operation *is* suitable for carrying out within the project file.

After the spectacular effects achievable with 3D Sectioning, the result may seem a little disappointing. This is because it is very literally a section and not a Sectional Elevation: nothing is shown of either the structure or 3D details in front of the section plane, 2D objects are ignored anyway. Proper roofs are shown, but floors, for some reason, are not.

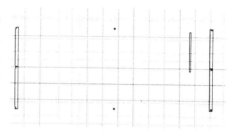

Nevertheless, it usually beats drawing sections from scratch. Don't be misled by the new layer being displayed initially in **Top** view: the objects are entirely 2-dimensional, and in fact Grouped together. Switch to **Top/Plan** to do proper drafting with the usual Smart Cursor aids.

Save your file.

◊

Drawing Analysis

One of MiniCad's best features is its ability to generate schedules automatically for you based on what you've drawn. There are two basic kinds: schedules for graphic information, e.g. areas, perimeters, lengths etc. that the program can work out itself from examining the objects on the drawing, and schedules for user-defined information, such as Manufacturer, Type, Finish, etc., i.e. information which the program has no way of knowing until you inform it with regards to each individual object. These two types of schedule are also created in slightly different ways. We'll examine each in turn.

Graphic Info Scheduling

A good example of this is a Room Areas Schedule. Earlier on, you may remember, we created polygons defining the each of the room areas and then assigned these to a special Class of their own. Although seeing them isn't necessary for the production of the schedule, let's make them visible again by making the Room Areas class our active class for a moment.

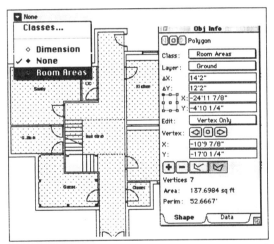 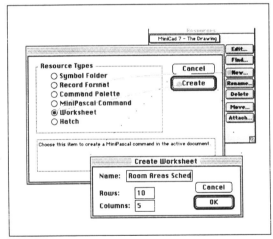

Click on any one—say, the Guest room—and call up its Obj Info palette. Note the variety of information the program 'knows' about this object (**Shape** information, as it calls it), which is constantly monitored and 'known' to the program, and can be accessed at any time.

Call up the Resource palette and click **New**.... In the dialog, choose **Worksheet** and Enter to **Create** it. Call it **Room Areas Schedule,** leave the default numbers of rows and columns and **OK**.

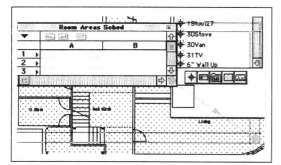

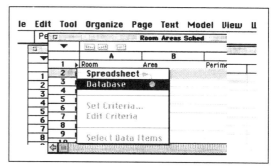

The worksheet appears open on the screen.

In contrast to previous versions, where it needed to be Opened manually from the Resources

Drag its resize box down and to the right to give yourself some elbow room.

In the cell A1, type Name, tab to B1, type Area, tab again and type Perimeter. These are only for our own benefit, as nominal column labels. Then click and hold on the **2** of the second row to get the pop-out list. Choose **Database**, which is to say that this row is to be something more than just an ordinary spreadsheet row.

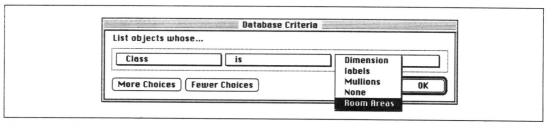

We get the dialog familiar to us from **Custom Selection...** and **Custom View...** Since the Room Area objects are in a Class of their own and we want to create a list just of them, select **Class** from the first pop-down list, **Room Areas** from the pop-down that appears on the right as a result, keep the second box as **is**, and **OK**.

Row 2 has sprouted sub-rows: as many as there are objects that have met the criterion we set, i.e. members of the Room Area class.

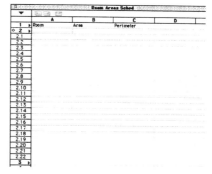

The program has already identified the items requested. It will now answer questions about them, posed to it in the form of formulas entered in the 'mother-row' cells, i.e. in A2, B2, C2, etc.

*The technical term for these is **Database Headers***

The subrows copy the 'mother row': type in a word or a number in A2 (what MiniCad would refer to as a **constant**), and all the 2.x cells in column A will repeat it. Type in a formula—i.e., something that starts with '='—and each sub-cell carries it out for the object it refers to. Thus,

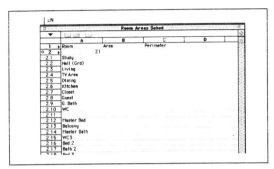

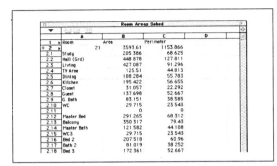

to get the Name of each object, type =N in cell A2, and Enter. MiniCad immediately returns the name that we entered for each room area in the first box of its **Data** section of its Obj Info palette.

In A2 itself, we get the number of objects that actually had a Name registered (in our case, one of the 22 didn't).

Type =Area in B2, and =Perim in C2 — Entering after each one—and you get the relevant figures for each of the Room Area objects.

®: *These are in the units defined for the file, so if you're working in mm, for example, you will need to modify the formulas: click on B2 and type /1000000 after =Area to get sq. m, and /1000 after =Perim in C2 to get metres.*

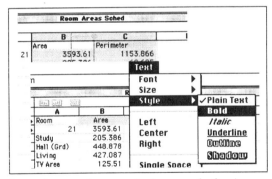

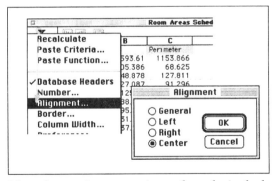

Once the numbers are in (or even before), you can do various things to clean up the worksheet, such as make the column labels Bold or otherwise directly from the main **Text** menu, or drag the boundary line between column headings to resize the column (select two columns to do them both at once), etc.

Most formatting operations, though, including numerical control of the column width, **Alignment...** of text within cells, Border lines (e.g., along the bottom of the label cells) etc. are carried out through the menu that pops down from the inverted arrowhead icon.

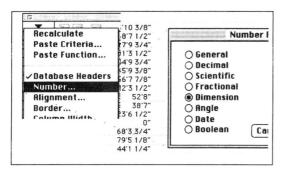 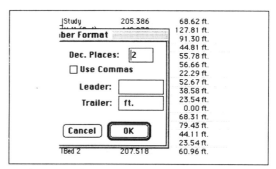

The **Number...** dialog, in particular, is of interest, as with it you can format linear lengths and distances automatically in the form *m'n"*, or if you prefer in **Decimal** form with a number of decimal places of your choice, with or without commas for 000's and millions, and/or text before (**Leader**) or after (**Trailer**) the figure.

The spreadsheet aspect of the worksheet kicks in when it comes to tying the information produced by such Database rows with figures in other cells:

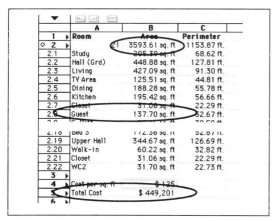 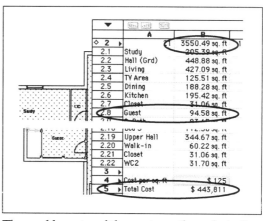

If in cell B4, for example, we type a figure for Cost per sq.ft [metre], then B5 can be calculated as =B4*B2

> *As in Excel, you can type this, or type just =*
> *click B4, type ★, and click B5*

The real beauty of the system, though, is that it is hotlinked to the drawing, so the moment one of the objects changes on the drawing, so do its measurements in the schedule and so every value linked to it.

> *This is one of MiniCad's most powerful features as a real-world tool.*

> *Note, however, that you do need to invoke **Recalculate** from the little spreadsheet pop-down for the changes to register.*

Area and Perim are but two of the functions or aspects that MiniCad can tell you about an object. =Length, for example, is very useful: it returns lengths of lines and walls. =XCenter and =YCenter provide the coordinates of an object's centerpoint in relation to the drawing's 0:0 point or **Origin**. =Count is self-explanatory.

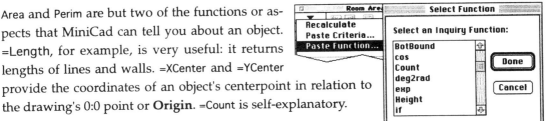

*Remember all Functions need an equals sign (=) typed before them to work—otherwise it's just a text constant that gets repeated down the subrows Note that **Height** does **not** mean the object's **Z** value , but rather the ΔY extent of a 2D object on the drawing. For an explanation of the others, see section 5 of the program's User's Guide.*

Sometimes you want to be more specific: instead of all the Room Areas, only those on the Ground Floor. Not a problem: you simply add more criteria to the List, either before the schedule is created or retroactively. In the case of the latter:

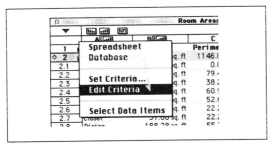

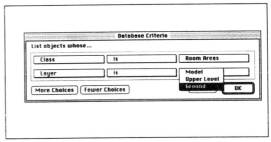

Click and hold on the row number of the Database to get the submenu, and choose **Edit Criteria...**

You get the familiar dialog for listing. Click **More Choices** to reveal a line for a second criterion, choose **Layer** from the first pop-up, and **Ground** from the one on the right. **OK**…

…– and the revised Schedule is shown, even without invoking **Recalculate**.

	Room		Area	Perimeter
1	Room		Area	Perimeter
2		10	1872.19 sq. ft	582.07 ft.
2.1			0.00 sq. ft	0.00 ft.
2.2	Closet		31.06 sq. ft	22.29 ft.
2.3	Dining		188.28 sq. ft	55.78 ft.
2.4	G. Bath		83.15 sq. ft	38.58 ft.
2.5	Guest		137.70 sq. ft	52.67 ft.
2.6	Hall (Grd)		448.88 sq. ft	127.81 ft.
2.7	Kitchen		195.42 sq. ft	56.66 ft.
2.8	Living		427.09 sq. ft	91.30 ft.
2.9	Study		205.39 sq. ft	68.62 ft.
2.10	TV Area		125.51 sq. ft	44.81 ft.
2.11	WC		29.72 sq. ft	23.54 ft.

Record Formats & Scheduling User-Defined Info

We saw how MiniCad relied on us to enter a Name for each object in order to show it in the worksheet, and how this was done via the Data panel of the Obj Info palette. For schedules of the kind needed for doors, windows and the like, that is also where we provide the input it needs on aspects such as Manufacturer, Type, Finish & code no., color, material and so on. Unlike Name, however, which we could just type in straight away, MiniCad asks that these attributes be arranged first in pre-defined sets. Such sets are referred to as **Record Formats**, and the idea is that once they're defined an object can then be assigned or Attached to the appropriate one, leaving us only to fill in the values that apply to each item individually.

The Record Formats available for us in the file are listed in the second box of the Data palette. MiniCad comes out of the box with two very common ones that are likely to be of use to almost everyone: Appliances , and Part Information. Click on either of these and see the list of attribute fields that it comprises. Appliances , for example, is a set of the following: Manufacturer, Type, Model, Color, Width, Price, Lead Time, and Description.

Some of the symbols which you may have imported from the program's Toolkit, for example, are tied to certain Record Formats. Click on one of them (e.g., 30Stove) and see for yourself.

• *When a symbol is Imported into a file, its Record Format comes along, too*

• *Items can be attached to more than one Record Format*

Making a new Record Format of your own (say, for Doors) is very easy:

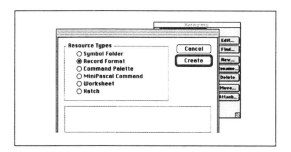

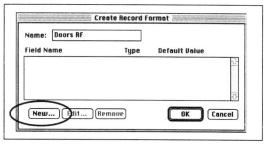

Click **New...** in the file's Resource palette to apply for a new Resource of the **Record Format** kind.

Name this one **Doors RF** and click **New...** to create the first attribute field

We're presented with the **Edit Field** dialog, where we tell it what kind of field we're after each case, and (optionally) the default value, i.e. the value that every object will take on the moment it is assigned to this Record Format.

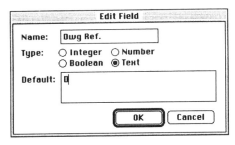

This will save on typing where all or nearly all items share the same value

Type **Dwg Ref.** for its name, and **D** as the default value. And **OK**

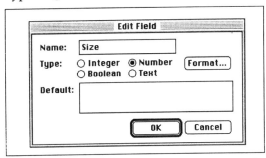

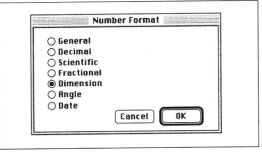

Repeat the process for the next field, **Size**, only this time click the **Number** radio button. This produces a **Format** button …

…–where we can ask it to apply:
- (@) the **Dimension** format ($m'n''$) or
- (®) **Decimal**, if you prefer

Carry on in this way, creating fields for Swing, Type, Finish, and Thickness, of which all are of the default **Text** type except Thickness, which should be **Number**. **OK** the **Create Record Format** dialog when finished.

With our Doors Record Format ready, we can now assign the various door instances to it. In the case of symbols already placed on the drawing this is done by selecting the instance(s) then ticking the Doors RF checkbox in the second section of the Obj Info Data panel, where all the file's Record Formats are listed.

With non-wall-based symbols you can batch-select them at once using the **Custom Selection...** *routine. With wall-based symbols like doors and windows you need to* Shift-*select them. Note that only the first one looks like it's selected: with the others only the wall boast handles—until, ironically, you deselect them afterwards (a screen redraw error)—but the assigning is carried out all the same. /...*

More about Worksheets

• Database subrow entries can be sorted alphabetically or from small to large by any column by clicking on the row number and dragging the small-to-large graph icon into the Database Header ('mother cell') of the relevant column.

The large-to-small graph icon of course sorts backwards (Z-A). A secondary sort is achieved by dragging the icon into the Database Header of another column. To unsort, simply drag the icon back to the icon pool.

		B	C
◇ 2 ▸	21	3550.49 sq. ft	1146.89 ft.
2.1		0.00 sq. ft	0.00 ft.
2.2	Balcony	350.32 sq. ft	79.43 ft.
2.3	Bath 2	81.02 sq. ft	38.25 ft.
2.4	Bed 2	207.52 sq. ft	60.96 ft.
2.5	Bed 3	172.36 sq. ft	52.67 ft.
2.6	Closet	31.06 sq. ft	22.29 ft.
2.7	Closet	31.06 sq. ft	22.29 ft.
2.8	Dining	188.28 sq. ft	55.78 ft.
2.9	G. Bath	83.15 sq. ft	38.58 ft.
2.10	Guest	94.58 sq. ft	45.69 ft.
2.11	Hall (Grd)	448.88 sq. ft	127.81 ft

•MiniCad distinguishes between a worksheet that is **Open** and one that is **On Drawing**. It is Open when you can enter data into it as we have done. On Drawing is when the worksheet appears as a graphic object that can be selected, moved (even fill-patterned) and printed with the rest of the drawing. It can only be one or the other at any one time. You decide by selecting it in the Resources palette and clicking the relevant button or checkbox.

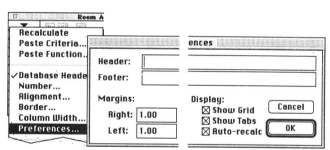

• If you do opt for On Drawing, the **Preferences...** dialog from the spreadsheet pop-down menu will allow you to turn off the Grid lines for a cleaner look, and/or add a Header or Footer, change margins, etc.

• Finally, if it's the actual figures you're interested in and want to work them up in Excel™ or some other spreadsheet, you can **Ex-port Worksheet** via the File menu, to create a separate file in one of a choice of suitable formats.

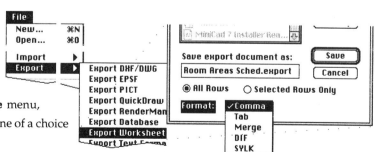

Normally, however, what will happen is that you will have the Record Format ready when you start drawing (it will be one of the Resources of your Stationery files), and you will 'attach' the symbol at master symbol level to it. Thereafter every instance placed on the drawing will 'know' it's assigned to a particular Record Format (or more than one, as the case may be)

This is done in the Resources palette: you select each symbol in turn from the list (you cannot Attach more than one master symbol at a time), click **Attach...** , and in the dialog that follows select the relevant Format(s) and check (tick) the **Attached** checkbox.

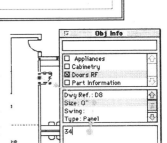

Attaching symbols to a record format at master symbol level also means that the fields' default values are automatically entered for every one of the symbol's instances placed on the drawing. All other values—or when the default value doesn't apply—are entered manually by selecting the instance(s) in question, then clicking on the relevant field in the third section of palette, and typing them in the fourth and final section, and either pressing Enter or clicking on the next field.

Alas, unlike assigning to Record Format, this is something you do have to do one-by-one in the case of wall-based instances already on the drawing

Do this now for all the door instances in the file. When finished, to create this kind of worksheet don't click **New...** in the Resources Palette but choose the new **Create Database Worksheet** (**Organize** menu).

In the dialog, call it **Doors Schedule**, choose **Objects with a record** from the first pop-up menu, **Doors RF** from the second, leave the Worksheet columns as they are, and **OK**...

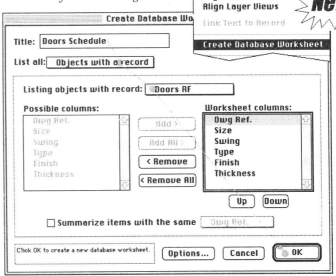

MiniCad produces the worksheet for you, with the Record Format's fields forming the column headings, row 2 defined as the appropriate Database, and the relevant formulas entered into each of the Database header cells. It remains for you only to click on the row number **2** and drag in the sort icon into the Dwg Ref. header cell to sort the list.

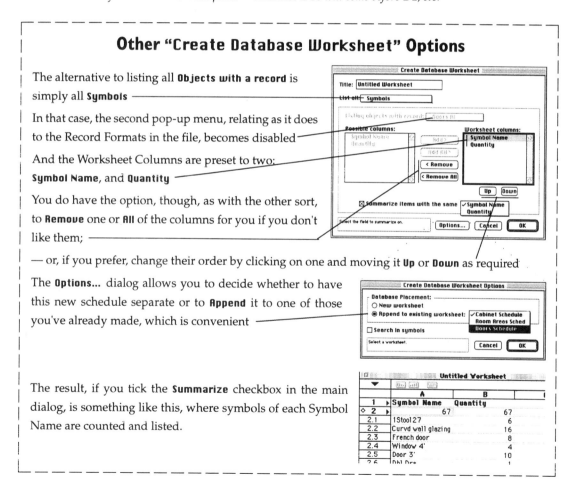

		Doors Schedule				
	A	B	C	D	E	F
1	Dwg Ref.	Size	Swing	Type	Finish	Thickness
◇ 2	11	33	11	11	11	11
2.1	D 1	5.333	R+L	6P Double	Veneer	2" solid
2.2	D 2	2.833	L	2P Single	Paint	1.25"
2.3	D 3	2.667	R	2P Single	Paint	1.25" hollow
2.4	D 4	2.667	R	2 Panel	Paint	1.25" solid
2.5	D 5	2.667	R	2P Single	Paint	1.25" hollow
2.6	D 6	2.667	L	2P Single	Paint	1.25" hollow
2.7	D 7	2.833	R	2P Single	Paint	1.25
2.8	D 8	2.667	L	2P Single	Paint	1.25" hollow
2.9	D 9	2.833	L	Glazed Single	Paint	1.25
2.10	D10	3	R	6P Single	Veneer	2" solid

Note

For the D numbers to sort properly, the single digits must have a space or zero placed before them in the Data panel— otherwise D10 will come before D2, etc.

Other "Create Database Worksheet" Options

The alternative to listing all **Objects with a record** is simply all **Symbols** ———————

In that case, the second pop-up menu, relating as it does to the Record Formats in the file, becomes disabled ——

And the Worksheet Columns are preset to two:

Symbol Name, and **Quantity** ——————

You do have the option, though, as with the other sort, to **Remove** one or **All** of the columns for you if you don't like them; ————————

— or, if you prefer, change their order by clicking on one and moving it **Up** or **Down** as required

The **Options...** dialog allows you to decide whether to have this new schedule separate or to **Append** it to one of those you've already made, which is convenient ———————

The result, if you tick the **Summarize** checkbox in the main dialog, is something like this, where symbols of each Symbol Name are counted and listed.

	A	B
1	Symbol Name	Quantity
◇ 2	67	67
2.1	1Stool 27	6
2.2	Curvd wall glazing	16
2.3	French door	8
2.4	Window 4'	4
2.5	Door 3'	10
2.6	Dbl Dre	1

Automatic Labelling (Linking Text to Record)

Assigning records to symbol instances has another big benefit. Instead of laboriously typing text labels next to each of the instances on the drawing, we can have the program do it for us, based on the value typed in one of the fields of the item's Record Format (which is a lot easier). Staying with the doors as our example:

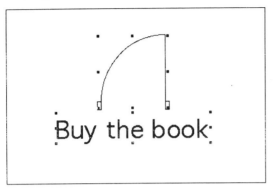

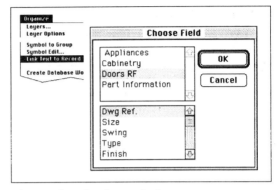

Use the Symbol Insertion Tool to place a new instance of our Door symbol in a blank part of the drawing, and type a bit of text (doesn't matter what) next to it, in the font, style, and relative position you would like applied to the actual label.

Then select both, and choose **Link Text to Record** (**Organize**). The program asks which field of which Record Format do we want to Link to. Click **Doors RF** from the top list, **Dwg Ref.** from the bottom one, & **OK**

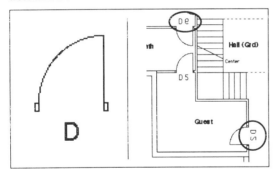

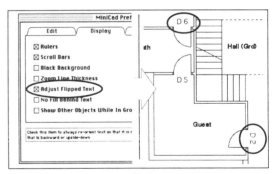

The text we typed earlier for the new instance is replaced with the default text of the Dwg Ref field of the Doors record format. More to the point, all existing instances of the same symbol have taken on their respective Dwg. Ref. values. But some labels are flipped, because

their instances were when placed. Not a problem: in the **MiniCad Preferences...**, **Display** panel, turn on **Adjust Flipped Text**. **OK** that, and back in the drawing—after a forced redraw (click on the drawing with the Pan Tool), the text is fixed.

124

ARCHITECTURAL DRAFTING IN MINICAD 7

As with the worksheet, the relationship is dynamic: change the value in the instance's Record, and it changes on the drawing as soon as you Enter or click on another field. Magic.

Note that the panel sizes are now modifiable by click-and-drag

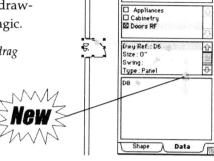

Remember that **Link Text to Record** is, in fact, a method of inserting parametric text (i.e. one whose value you can vary from one instance to the next on the drawing, but of a consistent form and position) into the 'body' of the master symbol. Should you ever want to change the attributes of this text or its position—or even to remove it completely—simply Edit the symbol's **2D** component as per usual.

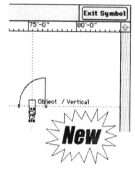

In contrast to previous versions, the text element is not an invisible placeholder but represented by the default value, making it easier to edit.

◊

Out & About

Site Plans

These days survey maps are more likely than not to be provided electronically — as AutoCad drawings or DXF exports thereof. In such cases, MiniCad's ability to **Import DXF/DWG** (**File** menu: **Import**) does the trick.

> *For the lowdown on importing & exporting DXF and the issues re AutoCad data, see Dave Weber's "DXF Made Easy". See the Qualum website* (http://qualum.com/) *for the URL.*

Often, however, one needs to bring in a drawing that is hard copy, such as a map or a sketch that was done by hand. In these cases, one scans in the drawing, saves it in PICT format (Macintosh) or .BMP (Windows).

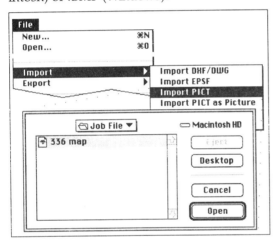

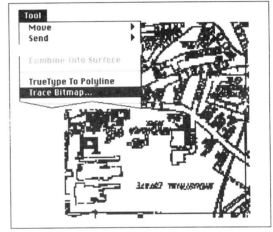

Assuming this is the case, you may Import it (**File** menu) through the **Import PICT** [BMP] option from the submenu pop-out. Locate the file and double-click on it to bring it in.

Select the imported file and choose **Trace Bitmap...** (**Tool** menu). The operation will take a few moments, depending on the image complexity and the specs of your machine.

- **Import PICT as Picture** *will not work for our purposes: this makes it unTraceable*

- *For best results, observe the following:*
  - *In the scanning software or a utility like GraphicConverter™, 'clean up' the scanned image by removing all superfluous pixel information before saving*
  - *Use a new or 'Jotting Pad' file for importing, and transfer to the drawing file after Tracing and processing*
  - *Set your scale to one similar to that of the hard copy <u>before</u> importing*

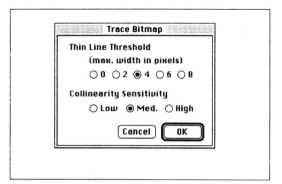

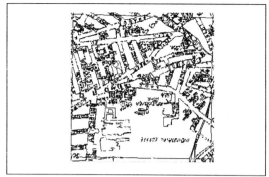

The higher the settings, the more 'literally' the program interprets every smudge and imperfection in the scanned lines. Experiment a bit, but start with the default settings.

Whichever way you play it, the result may well be a bit of a mess, unless the original was exceptionally 'clean'. In which case, a manual trace may be a good idea after all.

The exercise wasn't for nothing, though because, unlike the bitmap image, the traced file will be visible when viewed from another layer when **Layer Options** is set to **Gray Others** mode. Which is what we do now.

Also in preparation, as a new default pen setting (i.e., while nothing is selected on the drawing) choose a dark blue from the pen color palette and a thicker line than usual.

The better to distinguish what we're tracing from the underlying image

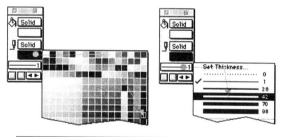

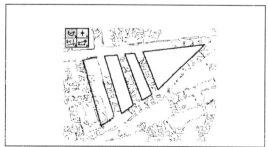

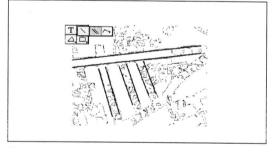

Depending on the type of site it is, you may wish to use a single-line polygon or the Polyline Tool to trace out the blocks…

But for urban sites, you may find the Double Line Tool (at the appropriate setting) preferable as with it you can just define short sections…

Custom Tool/Attributes: Drafting's Answer to Text Styles

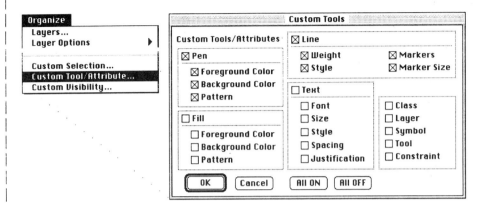

Like its sister Custom… menu items, **Custom Tool/Attributes…** produces timesaving Commands. These are designed to enable you to switch instantly between different tool settings as regards pen, fill, line, text… — well, you can read.

It does so by taking a snapshot of the current settings—or, to be more precise, those that you want preserving—for future use

In the above illustration, for example, we've asked it to note the current pen settings.

The dialog itself looks nothing like the other Custom… dialogs, but when you **OK** it, you get the same request to name the Command.

The resulting Command is added to your Commands palette and, by double-clicking on it, you should return to the settings recorded at the time.

A major but often-overlooked use of this facility is in creating Commands for different 'styles' of wall settings.

Simply set the Wall Preferences to what you want, call up **Custom Tool/At-tribute…**, and tick the **Tool** checkbox in the dialog (and any other attributes that you might want to keep, like Pen color or Line thickness), and name the Command accordingly. Remember that, as Resources, these Commands can be imported into other files, so you can add them to your Stationery.

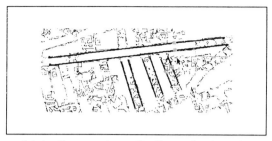

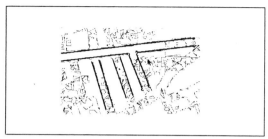

and join them automatically at the junctions, by selecting the relevant four lines each time... and choosing Join from the Tool menu or pressing ⌘ J [Ctrl+J]

It then remains only to reconcile the scale of the imported map with that of the traced image:

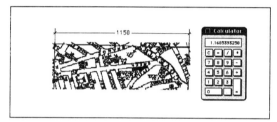

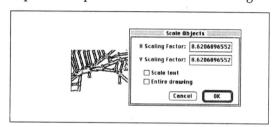

Dimension (i.e., ask what MiniCad 'thinks' is) a known distance on the imported map. Then call up the Calculator and work out the ration by which the traced drawing must be enlarged or reduced to achieve the same distance, and **Copy** the result to memory

Now **Select All** (⌘ A [Ctrl+A]—**Edit** menu) the traced map lines, choose **Scale Objects...** (**Tool**), **Paste** in the result from the Calculator in both the **X** and **Y** fields, and **OK**. The result should now be ready to transfer to your main drawing file.

After pasting it into a layer of its own at the same scale as those of the building, we are ready to use some of MiniCad's other tools:

With the **Move Page Tool**, for example (sidekick to the Pan Tool) we can shift the drawing on all its layers at once in relation to the printed sheet outline

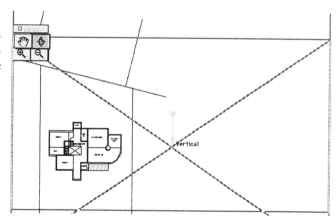

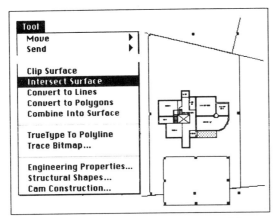

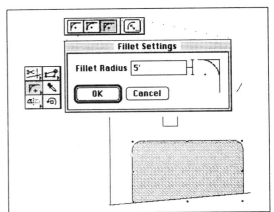

With the Ground Plan set to **Normal** and Layer Options to **Show/Snap Others**, a driveway can be created by **Intersect**ing the **Surface** of a suitable rectangle with that of the site itself, producing the required shape as a separate, new polygon.

With the **Fillet Tool** set to the appropriate radius through its Preferences dialog, once round the corners by simply click-and-dragging from one side of the corner to the other.

The effect is the same as using the Reshape Tool in its Change vertex mode set to Radial Arc. Unlike Reshape, though, is it works on lines as well as polygon corners

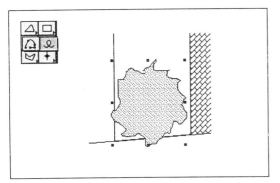

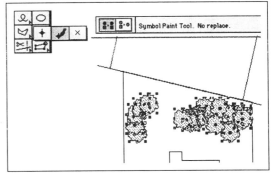

Another likely feature at this juncture is the **Freehand Tool**—great for greenery

But easy does it: the slower you draw with it, the more the object will have. Turn the result into a symbol to minimize the memory overhead

A similar freedom is possible with the **Symbol Paint Tool** (brother of -Insert), which allows instances of the current active symbol to be distributed with broad, painting-like strokes, offering a 'natural', unregimented look appropriate for clusters of trees and shrubs.

It has two modes, the second of which is supposed to replace symbols passed over by the cursor (presumably to facilitate 'mixed species' collections). I haven't been able to discern any difference in operation.

For a more controlled placement, try the **Duplicate Along Path Tool**—partner to the Mirror Tool. As its name suggests, this allows you to make multiple copies of any selected object—not just symbols—along a path. It has two modes:

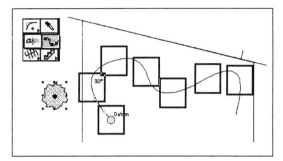

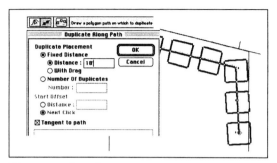

The default—Click on path object and then drag in duplicate direction—requires you to have a predrawn path object (polyline), on which you click where you want to start the series. It then varies the distance between the duplicates by the distance you drag after the initial click.

The second option—Drag a polygon path on which to duplicate selection—offers more on-the-fly control, but requires you first to enter the desired offset distance between the instances in the **Duplicate Along Path** dialog, and limits you to a straight-section polyline path.

As with Duplicate Symbol in Wall, neither mode requires you to start from the selected object

 The **Offset Tool** must be *the* dream tool for designers of Japanese pebble gardens, but it has more mundane applications for us ordinary folk, too. It provides parallel offsets to selected polygons, polylines, circles, arcs—in fact, any surface area object. It does so in one of two modes:

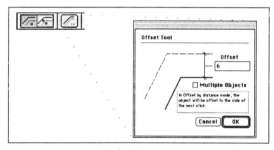

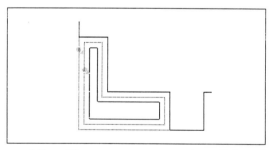

Offset by distance (default) requires you first to enter the desired offset in the tool's dialog…

…while with Offset to a point, you just click and drag to the point you want, with the previous offset acting as the new selected object.

◊

Other Tools & Menus

Part of knowing anything well is knowing which parts of it are important and which less so. The fact that we have come this far and yet there still remains a small collection of menus and tools that we haven't discussed yet is testimony to the depth of MiniCad as an application—but it also demonstrates how much is possible in a typical architectural context without using every single feature available (in other disciplines, of course, the mix of tools and priorities—particularly in 3D—may be different). Rather than thinking up ways of accommodating these remaining features in our scenario, which would feel forced and not truly integral to the plot, let's just review them here on their own:

2D Tools

Quarter Arc Tool
Neighbor to the Radial Arc, this produces quarter-ellipses.

Rotated Rectangle Tool
Devised to save you having to create an orthogonal rectangle and then rotating it. You first draw the base, then drag out the rest.

Regular Polygon Tool

For those situations when only a hexagon/octagon/...*n*-agon will do.

Three modes: Inscribed (center-to-vertex), Circumscribed (Center-to-mid-side), and Edge-drawn (draw a side, and the rest follows), respectively.

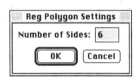

The default number of sides is 6—if you want different, change it in its Settings dialog

Trim Tool
Takes a little getting used to, as it works by clicking on the *non*-selected objects using the selected object(s) as the scalpel(s). The bit you click on is removed. Works on lines and surface-area objects, even when these are in front of the cutting object.

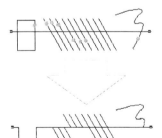

Including ellipses, now, I'm happy to report

Extend Tool

From the Trim Tool series, this extends lines to reach a line or object surface. Useful in constructing section and elevation drawings.

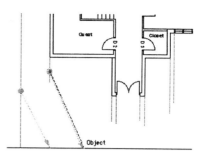

In default mode, you click-drag from the line to the line or surface it is supposed to extend to (neither of them needs to be selected—as in Fillets). In the second mode, the target line or surface is preselected, and the lines to be extended to it are clicked on one by one.

Resize Tool

First of the alternatives to the Reshape Tool, this carries out a rapid resizing of any selected 2D object or collection of objects.

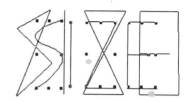

Different from ordinary resizing in that it's much faster, the object handles are not involved, and anywhere you click first can act as the fixed point.

Someone must have a use for it.

Shear Tool

Third in the Reshape series, this also uses your first click as a fulcrum point, but in this case to skew the selected object(s). Useful in creating the occasional false isometric of details.

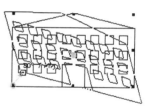

Chamfer Tool

Sister to the Fillet Tool, and works exactly the same way.

Property Bounds Tool

This provides you with the means with which to enter them to recreate the site accurately. Click to mark the starting point, then enter the figures for each line or curve, giving distance, bearing and radius as applicable, and **Apply**ing as you go, until **Done**.

Note: All angles are measured in relation to the starting point, not your last click

Number Stamp Tool

A timesaving device to automate the production of serial labelling of construction grid lines and the like. Before use, choose an appropriate default font size and style, and note roughly how big the label shape needs to be.

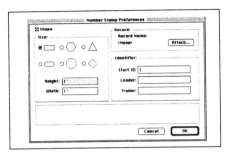

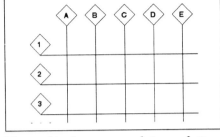

Then click the tool's Mode Preferences button to state the shape and size of the box, and the starting ID. Back in the drawing, click to place each consecutive label.

The tool is clever enough to use letters as well as numbers—but as for the shape's placement point, you can have any you like as long as it's the bottom one. But you can relocate them easily.

The reference in the dialog to Attaching the shapes to a Record is intriguing, but its implementation is unclear, since the labels produced are ordinary Groups, not symbol instances, as they would need to be to allow Linking Text to Record.

Revision Tool

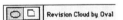

Creates a Group of radial arcs to produce a cloudlike shape suitable for highlighting revisions. Between the two modes—by Oval (created like an ellipse), and by Polygon—there is no contest: the latter is slow and produces an unattractive result with an oversized footprint that tends bizarrely also to 'capture' other objects in its orbit.

Fancy Doors

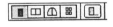

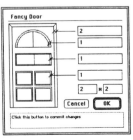

A well-intentioned macro that should make light work of producing panel doors but shoots itself in the foot by breaking the task down into individual, uncoordinated components instead of providing a comprehensive, one-stop dialog for an integrated design. Ah well.

Shutters Tool

No redundant trips to the Mode Bar with this one: just double-click to launch its settings dialog and set the slat and frame dimensions required. Works simply and well.

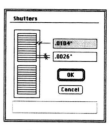

®: *The default figures are in inches: adjust if you are working in metric*

3D Tools

Light Creation Tool

By default, a single Directional (=Sun-like) source of light is created the first time you Render in any layer (all of which appear in the Model Linked to them). With MiniCad's ability to export the model in QuickDraw 3D format (*see below*), it makes sense to take advantage of the latter's facility to contain information on a model's illumination, so that this doesn't have to be done in the destination rendering program. Consequently, you can now create light sources of your own, each of which can be either **Directional**, **Point**, or **Spot** in character.

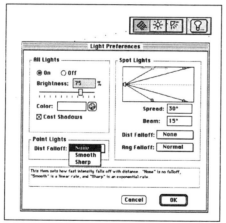

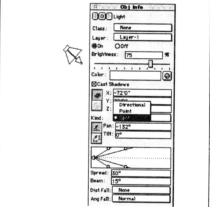

The decision as to which type and its attributes can be made at creation stage through choosing the appropriate Mode, or at any time later through the light object's Obj Info palette, after selecting the object

In fact, the Obj Info palette offers the same options and then some.

MiniCad demands that you place lights only in one of the 3D views, i.e. not in

Top/Plan. If you place it while in one of the Isometric views, though, you have no idea where it really is. So, for predictable results, always place the lights in

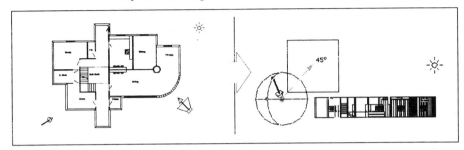

one of the orthogonal views (e.g. **Top**) check and move as required in the other.

 Of the three types, Directional lights are the most finicky to handle: to move one you must click on the precise center of its enclosing 'globe'. Once they're placed, you may find an Isometric view gives the most control when manually modifying the angle or azimuth (compass direction), each of which has its own special handle.

Remember, if you find the light objects distracting, there's no need to delete them: simply have them turned off—during wireframe or at all times—in the **Display** panel of the **MiniCad Preferences** dialog.

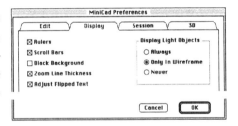

See discussions below on **Export>QuickDraw3D** *and* **Set Sun Position... on** *how to do shadow-casting & heliographic studies*

3D Extruded Rectangle
Produces rectangular boxes made of 3D flat polygons similar to those of a 3D Extruded Polygon (*see below*).

3D Polygon
As we saw when making hybrid symbols, a 3D polygon is one that may figure in the file's 3D model even though it has no thickness. Useful for creating flat features on 3D objects (e.g. on pediments). Define the surface it is to be created on as the current working plane before drawing.

3D Extruded Polygon

Not, as you might think, merely a 3D Polygon which is extruded at the same time, but a deceptive creator of ready-made collections of 3D Polygons, each of which is individually editable:

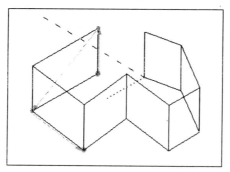 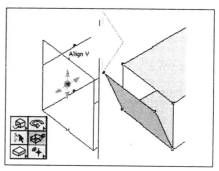

Procedurally, the extrusion dimension is defined with the first click-drag, not the last. Double click to finish. **Edit Group** in the usual fashion and see how each of the polygons can, with the Re-shape 3D Tool, be resized, pulled out of the vertical, or deleted, revealing the hollow structure inside.

Rotate View Tool

Turns the active part of the screen in a virtual trackball, providing complete freedom in rotating the view of the 3D model in all 3 dimensions, depending on which part of the screen the cursor is. You can toggle between the modes by pressing U, but as with its stablemate the Flyover Tool, the most predictable results are when you use the first mode, Rotate about center of the selected object(s). The two rightmost buttons turn the view 30° at a time.

Symbol Insert 3D

Works just like its 2D counterpart, though of course only on symbols with 3D aspects . Insertion can take place in any orthogonal (non-perspective) 3D view.

Mirror 3D Tool

Works much like its 2D counterpart, with similar option to duplicate at the same time or not. The 'mirror', as you would expect, lies perpendicular through the current working plane.

Rotate 3D Tool

Like Mirror 3D, this works only in one of the 3D views (i.e., not in **Top/Plan**), and is analogous to its 2D equivalent (including the option of duplicating at the same time). However, it has an additional Mode:

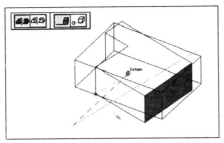

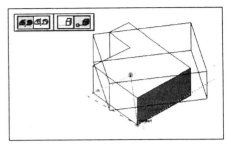

In the default mode it works in the familiar manner: you click to set the center of rotation, drag-and-click out the lever, and rotate (always on the current working plane).

The other mode is a tad more complicated: after setting the rotation lever, you click again (rather than rotate) to set the point where the lever should end. The object then jumps to it.

Align Plane Tool

'Stick This On This' is too informal for a tool name, but it describes its purpose more graphically. It is the answer to the question how to place one 3D object precisely on the designated surface of another. It works by defining the target surface as the current Working Plane, then clicking on the desired surface (or, in Wireframe mode, on three points defining it) of the object to be placed on it. The second is then placed on the first. The order in which you click, however, is crucial: for the most predictable results, define the working surface by clicking

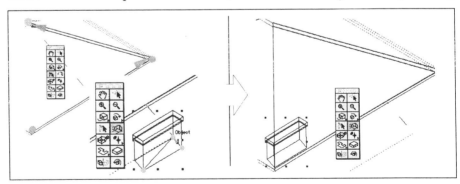

on its two base vertices first, and duplicate that order with the object to be placed. This way, the Alignment is made while preserving the object's orientation, which otherwise would not be the case.

File

(File:)

Revert To Saved

Revert to Saved: As the name suggests, this takes you back to the last saved version of the file. Used as a last resort when you've tried to fix things but they have gone so badly wrong that you'd rather start again where you left off. Another good reason (if such was needed) to save whenever you've completed something that's gone right.

Import
Export

Import: Apart from **PICT, PICT as Picture** which we discussed earlier, the other formats recognized for Importing are:

• **DXF/DWG**: The issue of using and manipulating drawings from surveyors and other consultants is much less of a problem as of this version given MiniCad's ability to read, edit & save AutoCad drawings in native (DWG) format and not just DXF (Digital eXchange Format)

• **EPSF** (Encapsulated Postscript Format): For bringing in logos and other elements of graphic design that are typically produced in *Illustrator*™, *Freehand*™, etc. without loss of their scale-independent resolution.

• **Text Format** : Nothing to do with helping you bring specification data into your drawings (for that you use good old-fashioned **Cut**-'n-**Paste** or simply type), but a means of reconstructing MiniCad files that may have been corrupted or of versions too old for v7 to **Open...** straight off the bat. You export it from the original file as Text, then import it here. Always use a blank, unformatted file for the purpose.

Also good for importing macros of previous versions

• **Worksheet**: Worksheets in other MiniCad files can of course be accessed through the Resources palette, but this allows you to bring in worksheets saved in common spreadsheet exchange formats such as comma-delimited, tab-delimited, DIS or SYLK. Can be used with active drawing files, but open up a new Worksheet within the file to receive the data into.

Export

Export options cover roughly the same ground as Import, with the addition of:

• **QuickDraw 3D**: Also known as 'metafile', this is a new format developed by Apple for generic exchange of 3D objects between Macintosh, Windows and Unix. Includes information on the model's geometry (including convertible measurement information), and lightsource and shading settings (if applicable). The QuickDraw 3D extension (available from Apple and other sources online) must be installed in your System before you can Export in it.

> *To include a light source in the exported file, render the model with one of the shaded option first. Incidentally, with the QuickDraw 3D extension, you can also Render with it — see box, right*

• **Renderman**: Also known as RIB (Renderman Interface Bytestream), this format requires the PixarLibsComp extension to be installed first. Used for exporting to programs such as *Showplace*™ where it may be rendered to a high level, using cues provided by the patterns and pen colors used in the MiniCad file. Offers special treatment options as regards the shading of individual sides of (true) walls, roofs and floors.

• **Database**: Refers in fact to the information in objects' Records. The resulting file can be opened in a spreadsheet or a word processor for viewing in a table format.

• **MiniCad 6**: Instead of a Save As... function for the same purpose.

(**Edit** menu:)

Paste as Picture does just that, to objects copied to memory (Clipboard). Good for situations where you would like to carry out operations such as **Trace Bitmap...** on an item which isn't in PICT [BMP] format and so cannot be Imported that way.

Clear—unlike **Cut**—removes the selected item(s) from the file without storing it in memory or Clipboard. Only **Revert to Saved** can bring it back.

On QuickDraw 3D Rendering within MiniCad

We saw earlier how we can create and edit new light sources in a MiniCad model, and we now know that this information is preserved when Exporting it in QuickDraw 3D format.

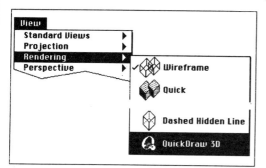

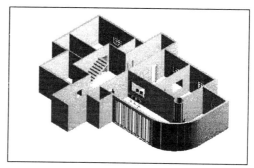

Well, if you can **Export** it, it means you have QD3D installed in your system, which means you can also Render it with the QuickDraw 3D option that is now added to the **Rendering** sub-menu.

The result is a textured model that takes into account the various light sources that have been placed. It is also remarkably fast, thanks to efficiency of the QD3D renderer, so you can easily use it instead of **Shaded Solid** or **Final Shaded** options for ad hoc evaluations as you design.

For a free copy of the latest version of QD3D (Mac or Windows) go to http://quickdraw3d.apple.com/

It gets better: MiniCad's QD3D-awareness also means that 3rd-party plug-in renderers will offer still higher levels of rendering— including the Holy Grail of shadow-casting *within the program* so that you no longer need to delay your gratification through Exporting and fiddling about in other programs. The first of these— **LightWorks SuperLite**—has just come out and is available for free download in demo version ($49 to buy) from http://www.lightwork.com

To activate any such plug-in once it is installed, call up **Document Preferences...** (**QD3D** panel) and choose it from the **Rendering Engine** pop-down menu. Then **OK** the dialog and Render the model by QD3D as before.

It's fun, but be warned: this kind of rendering takes a lot more time, and a lot more memory.

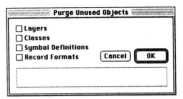

Purge Unused Objects... is a housekeeping operation you would typically invoke towards completion of a file or a significant part of it. It removes (per your choice in the dialog that follows) layers or classes that are completely empty and master symbols and/or Record Formats that have not been used.

Particularly relevant where the file was launched from a comprehensive Stationery file with the full complement of the symbols, formats, layers etc. of the practice, some of which were not needed. The operation is irreversible, so you are asked to confirm before it goes ahead.

Edit Attributes... provides a one-stop shop for customizing various defaults settings for:

• **Arrow Heads...**: works like the arrowhead dialog reached through the Fill Attributes palette, only providing for new default sizes and shapes for all types of line markers

• **Color Palette...**: Don't like the range of colors in the color palette?

Make your own, by modifying or completely replacing the color squares with new ones of your choice (even in the reserved selection, if you un**Lock** them)

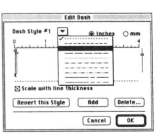

• **Dash Styles...**: This allows you to modify any of the existing choice of dashed lines in the Fill Attributes, add to it or delete from it. As well as varying the lengths of dashes or the spaces between them, you can add new dash patterns to a given line by click-and-dragging the handle on the right into the mix.

• **Line Thickness...**: A particularly important part of any professional Stationery file setup, this enables you to assign specific pen sizes to each of the five pen thicknesses— in mm, Points, or Mils.

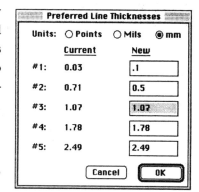

• **Patterns...**: Change the bitmap pattern of any of those from no. 36 onwards in the pattern pop-out—click in the square on the left to change a white (Background color) pixel to a black (Fore color) one, and vice versa. Revert to original if you change your mind. The resulting pattern is seen in the square on the right.

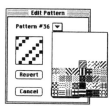

Smoothing applies to all vertices of a selected polygon/polyline(s) the effect achieved on individual vertices with the Reshape 2D Tool in its Convert vertex to Mode. The result, if applied to a single object as here, demonstrates the difference between Bézier (gray), Cubic (dotted) & Arc curves.

Lock makes the selected object(s) immune to deletion or modification of any kind until it is **Unlock**ed. Useful against inadvertent changes—if you can put up with the persistent reminder dialog that pops up every time you touch the locked item(s).

(Tool:)

Trim is an operation carried out with a surface object on lines: after selecting both, you choose the command, then click on any of the handles of the surface object. The lines get split along the boundaries of the surface object, ready for removal if required.

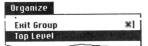

Truetype to Polyline is as good as its name in that it converts text of any Truetype font and size (but alas, only in Plain style) to fully editable polygonal objects.

As such, the letters (which are Grouped together in the process) can be filled…

—and/or Extruded, if required

Note

- *For Extrusion to work, letter objects with 'holes' in them will first need these to be proper holes by using them to Clip Surface the bit underneath them*
- *The quality of conversion of curves depends on the* **2D Conversion Res** *setting in* **MiniCad Preferences…**

Engineering Properties… is a hangover from the days when the Obj Info palette was a lot less informative about a selected object. Its sole unique advantage today: locating an object's center and marking it with a locus point.

(Organize:)

Top Level : In 'Russian Doll' situations—where you are editing a specific element in a Group within a Group within a Group (or within a Symbol)—this command takes you back in one step to the topmost level, i.e. the main drawing itself. Saves you having to **Exit Group** repeatedly.

Symbol Edit… —not to be confused with **Edit Symbol…** —is an important command that comes into play whenever we need to replace one or more instances of one symbol with another (but not all: for that you might as well change the symbol at **Edit Symbol…** level)

The procedure: select the instances to be replaced in the drawing, choose the command and, in the dialog that follows, click on **Choose Symbol** to call up the Resource palette and choose the replacing symbol, clicking on the appropriate insertion point in the right window of this dialog, and **OK**.

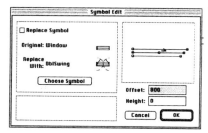

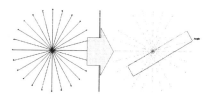

In the case of wall symbols, instances can only be replaced one by one, due to the impossibility of selecting more than one at a time.

The best results are when the two symbols share the same insertion point and orientation

(Page:)

Set Origin... : Your next click becomes the new (0:0) of the drawing file. Choosing the bottom left of the drawing sheet for this purpose has the advantage that all coordinates in the file become positive.

Guides: These are unobtrusive, grayed-out snap zones, created out of any 2D object (usually lines). Useful for situations where a special snap pattern is required, without the danger of

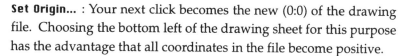

inadvertent deletions etc. that can come about from using ordinary 'live' objects to snap to. Once made, Guides can be deleted, hidden, shown etc. through this submenu.

Viewbar: The menu equivalents of the Viewbar tools at the bottom left of the drawing window, plus three common zoom views:
- **Normal:** the size objects would be when printed
- **Fit to Page:** the view zooms out to just accommodate the entire drawing area in the drawing window, &
- **Fit to Objects:** the window zooms in or out to just accommodate the selected object(s)

Tablet: Used to map the area of your digitizing tablet (of the ADB kind) to the drawing sheet on screen. You then **Set** the drawing's **Origin** to the bottom left corner of the tablet, and the drawing's (layer's) scale to that of the hard copy to be traced. Then choose this command to start drawing.

Requires the tablet software driver to be installed

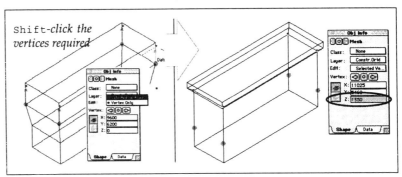

(**Model** menu:)

Convert to Mesh: Actually, like its neighbor just below it, this command turns selected a 3D object into collections of 3D polygons that can be individually Reshaped, deleted etc. In addition, however, it redefines it as a collection of vertices whose X-Y-Z coordinates can be changed even without having to invoke **Edit Group**: manually, using the 3D Selection Tool, or through the Object Info palette. What's more,

if you set the Object Info palette to Selected vertices, you can batch-edit or -drag several vertices at once. The result is best appreciated with **Multiple Extrude**d objects, where the increments were created equal but can now be changed as required. With the new facilities for adding, subtracting and Intersecting solids, though, the need for this command is less compelling.

Create Animation... : Formerly the **QuickTime** option of **Export**, this allows a walkthrough through or around the model to be saved as a QuickTime movie for future playback for presentation purposes. The walkthrough path can be either a default 'orbit' path around the object, or a custom route that you define. For the former, click the

ARCHITECTURAL DRAFTING IN MINICAD 7

first **Options** button to determine the center of orbit (on Ground Plane, Working Plane, or center of the selected object[s]). A **Preview** button at the bottom gives a very useful idea of the result in wireframe (but only for the Orbit-type, until you've defined a path):

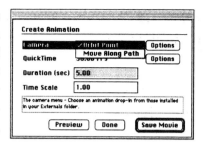

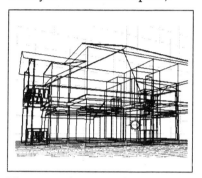

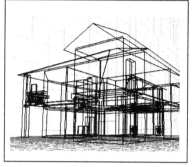

The second **Options** button reveals a dialog for the type and degree of compression of the QuickTime file. The choices you make here are largely governed by the tradeoff needed between quality and the size of the resulting file (which can reach dozens of Mbs very quickly): 30 frames per second, for example, is the professional video rate, but rates as low as 15fps are acceptable for most business presentations. The number of frames between **Key frames** (the Saved

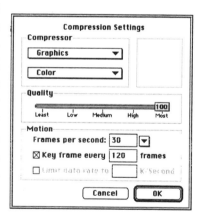

Views or Sheets you specify from the list in your file to create a particular **Animation sequence**) also needn't be anything as high as the default 120.

For a comprehensive and very clear explanation of the procedure, see pp 150-160 in the MiniCad User Manual.

Wall Framer: This is definitely the most fun of MiniCad 7's new functions, even if strictly speaking you may not need it, either because the builder knows his job well enough, or because your building is not of the wood frame type. It is also extraordinarily well thought out and comprehensive: by far the most elaborate and labor-saving of all MiniCad externals.

It first of all asks you to give a name to the model you have in mind, in case you will want to produce separate models for each of the layers (storeys) in the scheme. Say we call it **Ground.WF**

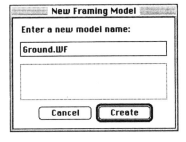

the 'WF' serving to distinguish it in the layer list, as we shall see

In the **Framing** dialog, you can choose which of the layers you wish to produce the model for, and what types of output. For our purposes, choose **Ground** and all three types of output.

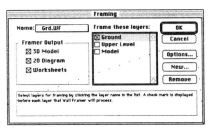

Click **Options** should you wish to change any of the default settings relating to the stud sizes or spacings, the dry wall sheet dimensions, etc.:

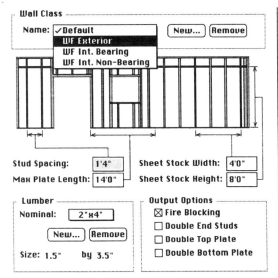

The result, after **OK**'ing the Framing dialog and a few moments processing, is a whole slew of goodies:

- Fully structured & completed schedules detailing takeoff and dimension information on the wall frames

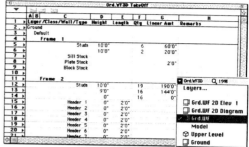

- A new layer with a 2D diagram of the frames in plan

- New Classes for all aspects of the frames' construction

- Another layer with fully-dimensioned 2D drawings of the frames in elevation, laid out across the whole width of the drawing area

- And yet another with a 3D model of the frame as set out in the 2D diagrams in accordance with your settings in the Framing dialog, ready for viewing and Rendering any way you like.

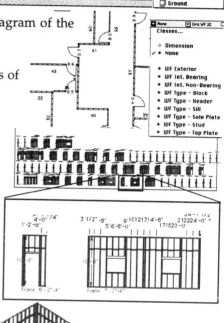

Enjoy.

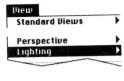

(**View** menu:)

Lighting.... This has a submenu of two items:

Set Layer Ambient... calls up a dialog for controlling the brightness and color of the ambient (non-direc-tional) light for the active layer, essen-tially the same in operation as the one we saw earlier for controlling those of individual light objects.

Set Sun Position...: Used in conjunction with QuickDraw 3D Export or within MiniCad using a suitable QD3D plug-in with shadow-cast-ing capabilities (*see above*), this provides for proper heliographic stud-ies using pre-computed sun positions for any location on earth at any time of year and time of day, taking into account even Daylight Savings Time. You just enter the figures.

The default settings refer to DiehlGraphsoft's location (natch)

Given the time need to render each scene within MiniCad, the im-

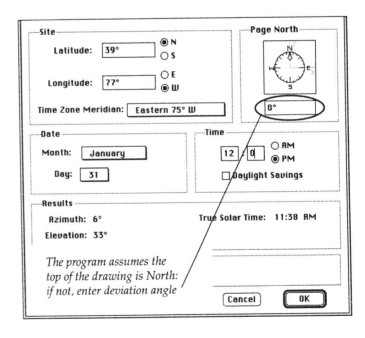

The program assumes the top of the drawing is North: if not, enter deviation angle

ages showing the progression of cast shadows are best Exported in QuickDraw 3D format for batching in a dedicated fast renderer.

Set 3D View ⌘0

Set 3D View: Best invoked when in **Top/Plan** or **Top** view, this provides greater control in creating perspective views than possible by simply stopping during a walkthrough sequence. Good for when you know exactly what point you wish to look at and from where, e.g. when creating the Saved Sheets (Views) to act as key frames in QuickTime animations (*see above*).

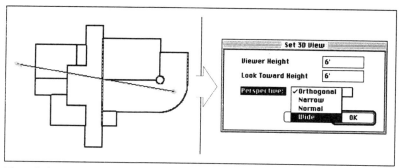

You define the two points by drawing an imaginary line from the observer to the target. The program then brings up a dialog where you type the heights of the observer and the point being looked at. The most natural result (i.e., vertical lines are vertical) are when the two figures are the same. Set **Perspective** is set to **Normal** or **Wide**.

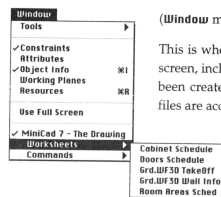

(**Window** menu:)

This is where you go to any palette that isn't currently open on the screen, including any Worksheets and Commands palettes that have been created—like all other palettes—of the active and other open files are accessed here.

◊

Appendix

"Dormer framing" (Toolkit:AEC:General:Samples)
Lower Left Isometric, rendered with Lightwork™ QuickDraw3D plug-in

Customizing your MiniCad interface using Overlay Edit

OverlayEdit is a small application , separate from MiniCad (available on the Mac platform only) that is installed in the same folder during the full MiniCad installation.

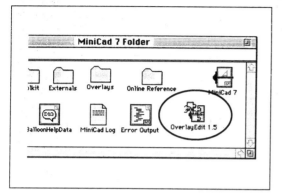

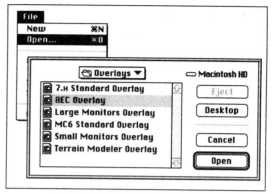

In the Finder [Desktop], double-click on its icon to launch it

Rather than make a **New** interface from scratch, ask to **Open** an existing one. In the dialog that follows, locate the Overlays folder, open it and double click on the **AEC Overlay** file.

You get a screen like this. I recommend you immediately **Save as...** this overlay under a different name, so nothing happens to the original should you make a mistake, and also so that you will have the option of two versions.

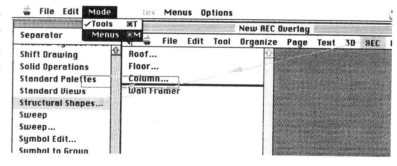

• Then select **Menus** from the **Mode** menu to get the list of possible menu items on the left.

• Click on the **AEC** menu of the existing AEC overlay to reveal its existing menu.

• Scroll down the list of menu items on the left, locate **Structural Shapes...** , and drag it in between **Column...** and **Wall Framer.**

The last two choices are purely of personal preference: I think as a menu command this item makes sense there, but you can choose any other menu and/or location to put it in

• Save your Overlay, quit the program, and back in MiniCad, choose your **New AEC Overlay** from the **File: Overlays** submenu, and call your uncle to confirm his name is now Bob.

There are other tricks you can do.

By choosing the **Option [Alt]** button at the bottom of the screen, you gain access to the variations of the menu commands that come up when that keyboard button is pressed within MiniCad. Simply drag the new command from the list onto an existing menu-item that currently doesn't have an **Option [Alt]** variation —i.e., is grayed out.

> *It makes sense to use a command that is logically related to the ordinary one—but the choice is yours.*

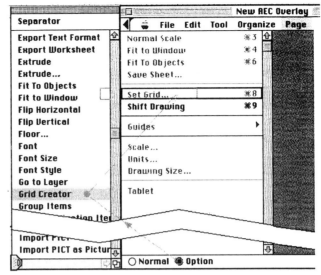

Customizing Tools

In Tools mode we can attend to other bugbears, such as fixing the single-key shortcuts to the 2D tools and Constraints in v.7.0.0 so that they tally with those set out in the basic MiniCad Help screens — or simply make a new set of your own.

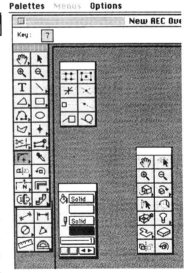

The procedure is simple: click on the tool in question, then type in the Key box at the top what key press you want. In many cases it may already be taken, in which case you will need to clear (delete) the key press of the offending tool first.

The idea behind the original MiniCad set is that they go from 1 through 9, starting from the **T**(ext) tool, which is as good a scheme as any. Before you assign key-presses, though, you might like to give some thought as to whether to keep the tools in the order that they are, or perhaps change them to something more to your liking.

To that end, you can select any of the tool palettes and resize them—making them longer or even three across instead of two—and drag in tools from the list on the left into the designated squares.

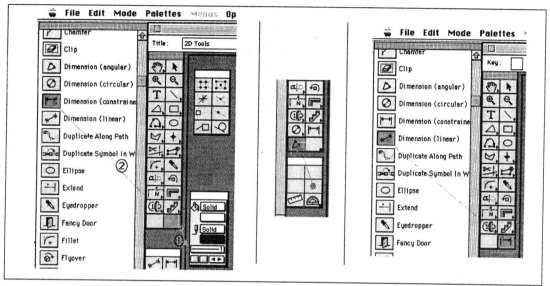

What's the betting that adding the dimensioning tools to the basic 2D palette is first on your list? You can, by the way, add them from the existing Dimensioning palette, but if you want more than one tool on a particular square—i.e., to make a pop-out series, then dragging from the list is the only option, as doing so from another palette simply replaces the existing tool on the square with the one being dragged.

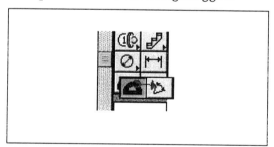

Having added a tool to an existing one, the last one brought it will be the default or first in the series. To change this, double-click on the square to reveal the series, then drag the one you want as default onto the first square.

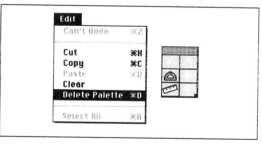

When finished 'looting' from an existing palette, select it and **Delete** it from the **Edit** menu.

There are many other options, including customizing the default screen size to suit the monitor you have. Using these facilities, you can produce an overlay such as the one I've developed for my own use, which is based on the AEC Overlay but where the menus now include **Structural Shapes...** and where the tools are rationalized and more tightly integrated, to wit:

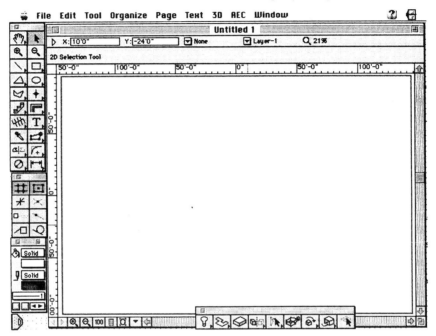

- The 2D tools are rearranged and grouped into logical pop-outs, with graphic primitive creator tools first, macro-based tools next, followed by tools for labelling and revising, manipulating and dimensioning
- Dimensioning tools group all Linear dimensioning (incl. the Ruler) in one pop-out series, the Circular and Angular types in another
- Related manipulative tools, such as Mirror, Rotate, and Duplicate along Path, all similarly grouped into single pop-out series
- The 3D Tools palette is rationalized and arranged along a single line at the bottom of the screen, still allowing scrolling on either side, with related creator and manipulative tools arranged in single pop-outs.

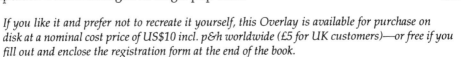

If you like it and prefer not to recreate it yourself, this Overlay is available for purchase on disk at a nominal cost price of US$10 incl. p&h worldwide (£5 for UK customers)—or free if you fill out and enclose the registration form at the end of the book.

Index

Index

Symbols

2D 118, 133, 145
  /3D (hybrid) objects 50, 72
  drawings 99
  in Cut 3D Section 113
  locus 64, 109
  Mirror Tool 137
  palette/tools 24, 30, 132. *See* 2D
  Reshape Tool 60, 63, 64, 65, 96,
    108, 130, 133, 143
  Rotate tool 107
  sections 113
  Selection Tool 38, 41, 66
  Symbol Insertion Tool 74, 137
  symbols 72
  vs. 3D symbols 76, 85
2D, 3D 37
  in stairs 57
3D
  Convert Res(olution) 106, 107
  details 105, 113, 138
  Extruded Polygon/Rect. 112, 136
  extrusion. *See* Extruding
  info, exchange of. *See* exporting: model
  Locus Tool 109
  Mirror Tool 137
  model 24, 72, 97, 99, 105, 137, 146, 149
  model, walkthroughs in. *See* Walkthrough:
    Tool
  palette/tools 24, 135
  polygons 136, 146
  QuickDraw-. *See* QuickDraw 3D
  Rendering options 20, 105. *See also* Rendering
  Reshape Tool 98, 137
  roofs. *See* roof
  Rotate Tool 137
  sections 112, 113
  Selection Tool 45, 46, 146
  Standard Views 137

Symbol Insertion Tool 137
symbols 72, 85
7.x Standard Overlay 17, 27, 49, 105

A

Add Solids 109, 146
Add Surface 60, 109
AEC
  Overlay 17, 27, 105, 155. *See also* Overlay:
    AEC
Align 96
  Layer Views 44
  Plane Tool 138
  text in worksheet 116
  with SmartCursor 31, 63, 64, 80, 90, 96
Alt key. *See* Option key
Angle 30
  constraining. *See* Constrain: Angle
  dimensioning 103. *See also* Dimensioning:
    angles
  of roofs 89, 90
angle 133
  of arrowheads 22
  of rotation. *See also* Rotate
  of Swept object segments 106
Animation
  , Create 146
ANSI. *See* ASME
applications
  , CAD 38, 99
  , draw-type 24, 28
  , Mac 39
  , other 13
arc 28, 131, 143

Excel™ 117, 121
Export
    formats 140
    QuickDraw 3D 140, 141, 150
    QuickTime 146
    RIB 140
    worksheet 121
exporting
    model 105, 140
Extend Tool 133
Extension Line 26
Extrude 35, 44, 54, 62, 63, 110
    , Multiple 108. *See also* Multiple Extrude
    converted text 144
    in symbol creation 77, 78, 82
Extrusion
    value in Multiple Extrude 109

F

feet & inches. *See* units: of measurement
fill
    cavity 52
    color 50
    pattern 28, 32, 34, 36, 49, 50, 52, 63, 66,
        71, 73, 90, 93, 99, 101, 121, 128, 142,
        143, 144
Fillet 133
    Tool 130, 133
Fit
    to Objects 145
    to Page 145
Floating Datum 21, 33, 64, 77, 81
Floor 60, 61, 106
    as 3D object 105, 107, 140
    as storey 93, 99
    editing 62
Floors
    in 2D Sections 113
Flyover Tool 97, 137
Fore(ground) color 58, 143
Freehand

objects 28
Tool 130
Front (Standard View) 106, 108. *See also* elevation

G

GA drawing 99
gable 91, 93, 98, 111
GraphicConverter™ 126
Grid
    , Construction. *See* Construction Grid
    in worksheet 121
Grid…
    , Set 77
Ground Plane 147
Group 34, 35, 39, 49, 54, 69, 76, 102,
        113, 134, 144
    , Edit 35, 62, 63, 75, 81, 106, 137, 144, 146
    , Symbol to 75. *See* Symbol to Group
    in Cut 2D Sections 113
Guides 145

H

Hatch 101
Height
    in Swept objects 107
    in worksheets 118
height 90, 99, 105. *See also* $Z/\Delta Z$
    of 3D column 107
    of roof 90, 92, 95
heliographic studies 150
Help file 27, 156
Hide
    page breaks 20
    polygon edges 65
    types of object 55

W

X

Y

Z

Registration Form

Thank you for buying this book! To help us improve and tailor future editions to your needs, please photocopy & complete the form below and return to the address on the back of this page — or fill it in at our website (http://qualum.com/). In return, you will receive advance notification of future editions, $45 (£30) off all Qualum training in MiniCad 7, and a copy of the Qualum AEC Overlay** (normally $10 / £5 incl. postage—*see Appendix*).

Your details are for our internal use only. We do not share customer information any other organization.

Name:_____ Co./Org. (if any):_____

Address (*incl. country*):_____

ND FOLD

_____

Tel.(*incl. area code*):_____ Fax.:_____

Email: _____

• Is this the first edition of *Architectural Drafting in MiniCad* that you've bought?   ❑ Yes ❑ No

• Would you be interested in MiniCad training or seminars by the author? _____

• Do you belong to a MiniCad User Group (*If so, which one*)? ❑ No ❑ Yes: _____

• Where did you buy this book? _____

• Was it recommended to you? If so, by whom?_____

• How does it compare to competing publications (*if known*)? _____

• What professional (computer-, design- or building-related) magazines do you read regularly?

_____

FOLD

• Which of the commercial MiniCad add-ons do you use (*if any*)?_____

• Which add-ons would you like to see covered in future editions of *A.D.i.M.*.(*if any*)? _____

• Are you interested in a copy of the Qualum AEC Overlay?   ❑Yes ❑No

• Please tell us your impressions of this book and how can it be improved (*continue overleaf if necessary*):

_____

_____

_____

_____

** Mac only

Registrations

Qualum Publishing

665 Finchley Road

London

NW2 2HN   United Kingdom

_____

(cont. from overleaf)